The Best You Can Be

A Teen's Guide to Fitness and Nutrition

The Science of Health: Youth and Well-Being

Taking Responsibility
A Teen's Guide to Contraception and Pregnancy

Staying Safe
A Teen's Guide to Sexually Transmitted Diseases

What Do I Have to Lose?
A Teen's Guide to Weight Management

Balancing Act
A Teen's Guide to Managing Stress

Surviving the Roller Coaster
A Teen's Guide to Coping with Moods

Clearing the Haze
A Teen's Guide to Smoking-Related Health Issues

Right on Schedule!
A Teen's Guide to Growth and Development

The Best You Can Be
A Teen's Guide to Fitness and Nutrition

The Silent Cry
A Teen's Guide to Escaping Self-Injury and Suicide

Breathe Easy!
A Teen's Guide to Allergies and Asthma

Can I Change the Way I Look?
A Teen's Guide to the Health Implications of
Cosmetic Surgery, Makeovers, and Beyond

Taking Care of Your Smile
A Teen's Guide to Dental Care

Dead on Their Feet
Teen Sleep Deprivation and Its Consequences

Dying for Acceptance
A Teen's Guide to Drug- and Alcohol-Related Health Issues

For All to See
A Teen's Guide to Healthy Skin

THE BEST YOU CAN BE

A Teen's Guide to Fitness and Nutrition

by Christopher Hovius

Mason Crest Publishers

Philadelphia

Mason Crest Publishers Inc.
370 Reed Road, Broomall, Pennsylvania 19008
(866) MCP-BOOK (toll free)
www.masoncrest.com

ISBN 1-59084-840-3 (series)

Library of Congress Cataloging-in-Publication Data

Hovius, Christopher.
  The best you can be : a teen's guide to fitness and nutrition / by Christopher Hovius.
       p. cm. — (Science of health)
  Includes bibliographical references and index.
  ISBN 1-59084-848-9
  1.   Physical fitness—Juvenile literature. 2.   Physical fitness for youth—Juvenile literature. 3.   Nutrition—Juvenile literature. 4. Teenagers—Nutrition—Juvenile literature. I. Title. II. Series.
  RA781.H66 2005
  613.7'043—dc22
                           2004012715
First printing.
1 2 3 4 5 6 7 8 9 10

Designed and produced by Harding House Publishing Service, Vestal, NY 13850.
Cover design by Benjamin Stewart and Michelle Bouch
Printed and bound in India.

This book is meant to educate and should not be used as an alternative to appropriate medical care. Its creators have made every effort to ensure that the information presented is accurate and up to date—but this book is not intended to substitute for the help and services of trained medical professionals.

CONTENTS

INTRODUCTION

by Dr. Sara Forman

You're not a little kid anymore. When you look in the mirror, you probably see a new person, someone who's taller, bigger, with a face that's starting to look more like an adult's than a child's. And the changes you're experiencing on the inside may be even more intense than the ones you see in the mirror. Your emotions are changing, your attitudes are changing, and even the way you think is changing. Your friends are probably more important to you than they used to be, and you no longer expect your parents to make all your decisions for you. You may be asking more questions and posing more challenges to the adults in your life. You might experiment with new identities—new ways of dressing, hairstyles, ways of talking—as you try to determine just who you really are. Your body is maturing sexually, giving you a whole new set of confusing and exciting feelings. Sorting out what is right and wrong for you may seem overwhelming.

Growth and development during adolescence is a multifaceted process involving every aspect of your being. It all happens so fast that it can be confusing and distressing. But this stage of your life is entirely normal. Every adult in your life made it through adolescence—and you will too.

7

But what exactly is adolescence? According to the American Heritage Dictionary, adolescence is "the period of physical and psychological development from the onset of puberty to maturity." What does this really mean?

In essence, adolescence is the time in our lives when the needs of childhood give way to the responsibilities of adulthood. According to psychologist Erik Erikson, these years are a time of separation and individuation. In other words, you are separating from your parents, becoming an individual in your own right. These are the years when you begin to make decisions on your own. You are becoming more self-reliant and less dependent on family members.

When medical professionals look at what's happening physically—what they refer to as the biological model—they define the teen years as a period of hormonal transformation toward sexual maturity, as well as a time of peak growth, second only to the growth during the months of infancy. This physical transformation from childhood to adulthood takes place under the influence of society's norms and social pressures; at the same time your body is changing, the people around you are expecting new things from you. This is what makes adolescence such a unique and challenging time.

Being a teenager in North America today is exciting yet stressful. For those who work with teens, whether by parenting them, educating them, or providing services to them, adolescence can be challenging as well. Youth are struggling with many messages from society and the media about how they should behave and who they should be. "Am I normal?" and "How do I fit in?" are often questions with which teens wrestle. They are facing decisions about their health such as how to take care of their bodies, whether to use drugs and alcohol, or whether to have sex.

This series of books on adolescents' health issues provides teens, their parents, their teachers, and all those who work with them accurate information and the tools to keep them safe and healthy. The topics include information about:

- normal growth
- social pressures
- emotional issues
- specific diseases to which adolescents are prone
- stressors facing youth today
- sexuality

The series is a dynamic set of books, which can be shared by youth and the adults who care for them. By providing this information to educate in these areas, these books will help build a foundation for readers so they can begin to work on improving the health and well-being of youth today.

1

SELF-ESTEEM

The Role That Feeling Good Plays in Our Health

Carlos approached the convenience store counter. Behind it, the clerk watched a car pull into the parking lot. Feeling self-conscious, Carlos ran his hand through his hair and hunched down. The clerk looked at Carlos and waited for him to speak. Avoiding eye contact, Carlos reached out, grabbed a chocolate bar, and slid it toward the clerk.

"That it?"

Instead of answering, Carlos turned to the magazine stand, picked up a copy of *Pro-Wrestling Weekly*, and laid it beside the chocolate bar. The clerk rang in the sale and handed Carlos his magazine, chocolate, and change.

"There you go, buddy, have a good one."

"Thanks," muttered Carlos. *Some guy*, he thought to himself, *telling me to have a good one*. As he headed for the door, he glimpsed his reflection in its glass. His image was warped, fattened, and three-feet tall. He pushed the door open and stepped outside into the chill. He felt the people in the nearby car staring at him, looking at his

If teens can balance the key board and the skate board—computer activities that provide intellectual stimulation with sports that provide physical exercise—they will be more apt to achieve good health.

arms—too weak—his legs—too short—and his stomach—too fat. Carlos's face flushed with shame. He wished he could hide.

Despite its current miserable state, Carlos's day had started differently. At breakfast, his mom congratulated him for the *third* time on his geography mark. And for most of the morning, he joked with his friends Ahmed and Frank. It wasn't until dressing in the locker room for gym class that things changed. That's when Wayne announced that Carlos had no muscles.

"You can't flex fat," Wayne yelled among a scattering of snickers. It didn't take much pressure to split fissures into Carlos's fragile confidence.

Now Carlos stared at the chocolate bar. *Part of the problem*, he said to himself. Looking at the magazine made him feel even worse. He knew he needed a change, but how could he ever look like the guys in the magazine? "Get mammoth pipes!" one advertisement read. "Want these huge abs? We'll show you how," another proclaimed. But Carlos knew from experience that the magazine's "fat-burning secrets" and "miracle workouts" were hard to stick to and never amounted to much. *I'll never be able to look this way*, Carlos thought. *Why even bother?*

Why Fitness and Nutrition Are Important

Have you ever felt guilty for indulging in a candy bar, felt ashamed of part of your body, or wished you could look like the people in magazines? If you're like most people, you could probably answer yes to at least one of these questions. Like Carlos, most people wish they could change at least one part of their bodies. Also like Carlos, many people turn to glossy magazines filled with tips on dieting, body building, and miracle makeovers in a quest to improve their bodies. But you don't have to look like a supermodel or body builder to be healthy and happy. In fact, as we will see later, images like these sometimes put beauty before health, and many people seeking to improve their bodies overlook the fundamentals of health and well-being: fitness and nutrition.

Fitness and good nutrition are the foundations upon which a healthy, happy life is built. Think, for a moment, about the last time you were sick. You probably felt exhausted, achy, unhappy, and couldn't concentrate on anything more than watching television. You probably couldn't wait to get well and felt extremely thankful when the illness finally ***abated***. Being unhealthy from poor nutrition and lack of exercise can be like having a low-grade illness all the time. Your energy will be low, your enthusiasm lacking, and concentration difficult. You might become so used to living this way that these bad feelings start to feel normal. If you began exercising and eating right, however, you would suddenly notice not only changes in your energy levels and physical strength but changes in your emotions and mental functioning as well.

Obviously, exercise and proper nutrients improve our physical health, but you might wonder how they can affect your emotional and mental well-being. Exercise and nutrients affect our minds and emotions in both physical and nonphysical ways. For example, nutrients like some types of vitamins can ward off depression. Similarly, during exercise our bodies release endorphins—chemicals that help improve one's mood. These physical reactions affect our mental and emotional functioning. Exercise

14

and good nutrition can also impact your mind and emotions in nonphysical ways by improving your self-esteem and body image.

Self-Esteem

Self-esteem is, very simply, the way you feel about yourself. If you feel confident, capable, and happy with yourself, you have high self-esteem. If, like Carlos, you feel ashamed of and dissatisfied with yourself, you might have low self-esteem. Having low self-esteem can make it difficult to succeed, or even to try, in areas where you have little confidence. When faced with a challenge, a person with low self-esteem—like Carlos—might think, *I can never do this. Why even bother?* A person with high self-esteem, on the other hand, might think, *Either I can do this, or I can give it my best shot.*

Your self-esteem has been in the making since the day you were born, and many factors affect it. Every positive comment you hear can boost your self-esteem. Every negative comment can take its toll. Every accomplishment, from learning to ride a bike to scoring well on a test, increases your self-esteem. Every failure undermines your positive feelings. No one can expect to go through life without ever experiencing negativity or failure. Hopefully, however, you can build positive self-esteem so that when negative things do happen, you are able to cope, dust yourself off, and try again.

The teenage years can be an especially difficult time for one's self-esteem. Your physical body is just one of the things that affect your self-esteem, but as a teenager, your body might suddenly seem more important than ever before. At this time in your life, your body is changing at an incredible pace, and many teens feel self-conscious and uncomfortable with these changes. At the same time that you're feeling so awkward about yourself, you are bombarded with **media** images of very thin supermodels, glamorous movie stars, and impossibly buff athletes. Mix these ingredients with the cocktail of **hormones** raging through your body, and the tumultuous emotions they can cause, and you have a recipe for self-esteem disaster. Low self-esteem in the teenage years is often related to poor body image.

BODY IMAGE

Body image is the way you see your physical body and the way you believe others see you. Like self-esteem, our body image develops over time in response to many experiences, and it changes throughout your lifetime. For example, if you play sports or engage in physical activities, you might see your body as strong, athletic, and capable. If you've never engaged in physical activity, you might think your body is weak and unable to do many things. A compliment on your looks will boost your body image. An unkind comment, like the jeer Carlos sustained from Wayne, can hurt your body image. It is extremely important to remember that your body image is not the way your body *actually* is, but rather the way you *think* your body is.

Many people in North America do not see their bodies as they really are; they have a distorted body image. When Carlos sees his reflection in the door, he thinks he looks short and fat. Many people see their bodies in a

Exercise can help you feel better about yourself.

The Best You Can Be

Everyone has a unique body. What's important is to keep yours in the best health possible.

similar way—as flawed, unattractive, or overweight when they are really none of these things. When we compare our bodies to the images we see in the media, it is hard not to see our bodies as flawed. In reality, however, it is often those *idealized* images of beauty that are actually distorted versions of what a "good" body is. What you see in magazines and on television is in almost all cases unattainable. It is what some people call the North American beauty myth, and it is created through professional makeup, clever lighting, airbrushing, digital enhancement, and in some cases, things as dangerous as starvation and *steroids*.

Body image is very important to your self-esteem, and one of the first steps toward developing a positive body image is being realistic about the human body. If you are dissatisfied with the way your body looks, you are in the majority. According to the National Eating Disorders Association, 80 percent of women are dissatisfied with their appearance. In addition, four out of five ten-year-old children fear being fat. *Psychology Today* reports that 53 percent of men are dissatisfied with their weight. Even a person who seems confident about her looks might actually be quite insecure about them. On the road to better body image and high self-esteem, it is important to remember that there is no universal standard of beauty.

If Barbie™ were an actual human being, she would wear a size 4. The average North American woman wears between sizes 11 and 14. Wearing a smaller size is no gauge of beauty. Did you know that Marilyn Monroe, a woman renowned for her beauty, sometimes wore a size 14?

The Best You Can Be

Everyone—including you—has a unique body. Far more important than how your body *looks* is how your body *feels*. Focusing on nutrition and fitness, rather than on looks, is an excellent way to reevaluate your attitude toward your body. When your goal is to get healthy, rather than to get skinny, buff, sexy, or whatever, you are on the road to complete physical, emotional, and mental well-being. When you're eating right, staying fit, and feeling healthy, you'll find that your body is great to be in, no matter what it looks like!

So is it bad to want to improve your looks? Of course not! But it is important to have balance. While there is nothing wrong with wanting to improve your physical appearance, there are many more reasons to stay healthy than just your looks. At this point in your life, understanding how your body works can build long-term confidence through good health. Poor nutrition now can impact your health long into the future. Being unfit when you're young can make it harder to get fit as an adult. Poor self-esteem at this stage in your life can hold you back in your future. Of course, it is never too late to start living healthfully, but if you begin now, the benefits will follow you throughout your life.

Throughout this book, establishing and maintaining good health will be discussed. You will notice a common theme prevailing throughout: the idea of balance—balancing the desire for looks with a desire for health, balancing the foods you know you should eat with the foods you want to eat, balancing exercise and hard work with rest and relaxation. Some of the information we'll look at may seem complicated and confusing. Furthermore, it might seem impossible to do everything right all of the time. As you read, remember, you're not a superhero. You're a person with habits, desires, and cravings. Sometimes you may feel tired, insecure, incapable, or overwhelmed. Just remember, no one needs to be a superhero to be healthy. Good health, a positive body image, and high self-esteem are things everyone can achieve.

2

TO KEEP YOU GOING

The Energy-Rich Nutrients

"Eat your vegetables
—or you won't grow up
to be big and strong."

"An apple a day keeps the
doctor away."

"You are what you eat."

We've all heard advice like this. In fact, we've probably heard it so many times that we don't really listen anymore. But in fact, your body's health relies on what you choose to eat. Choose to eat food that's rich in nutrients, and you will be more likely to be healthy and strong; choose to eat nothing but junk food and soda, and your body will have less of what it needs to be healthy. Nutrients—the substances in food that nourish our bodies in various ways—are the building blocks of good health.

There are many types of nutrients, and the wider range you select, the healthier you will be. Each person should receive about fifty different types of nutrients on any given day. Six of these nutrients are so important that they are called the *essential nutrients*. These are carbohydrates, fats, proteins, vitamins, minerals, and water.

Nutrients provide the substance to build bones, muscles, and other body tissues and supply the chemicals that *facilitate* important body functions. Three of these nutrients, carbohydrates, fats, and proteins, also provide the energy that keeps your body and mind running. In this chapter, we discuss food energy, carbohydrates, fats, and proteins in detail, consider some of the myths and facts associated with each of these things, and give hints for using these nutrients as part of a healthy lifestyle.

CALORIES: THE MEASUREMENT OF FOOD ENERGY

We measure the amount of energy in food with a unit called a Calorie. A Calorie is a thermal unit of energy; it is an amount of heat. Calorie with a capital "C" stands for *large calorie* or *kilogram calorie*. This is the type of Calorie used to measure energy in food. One Calorie is equal to the amount of energy it would take to heat one kilogram of water one degree Celsius. There is also a measurement known as a *small calorie*, or calorie with a lower-case "c." This type of calorie is used in chemistry, physics, and other disciplines that need to accurately measure tiny amounts of heat. A small calorie is the amount of heat it takes to heat one gram of water one degree Celsius. There are one thousand small calories in a single food Calorie.

Calorie Myth: *I should eat 2,000 calories a day.*
Truth: If you look at the nutrition information on food labels, you will usually see the phrase, "Based on a 2,000 Calorie diet." This is where many people get the idea that

25

they should eat 2,000 Calories per day. The truth is there is actually a range of Calories that should be consumed per day depending on your activity level, body size, age, and sex. The average eleven- to fourteen-year-old female needs 1,500 to 3,000 Calories daily, depending on her body type and activity level. Young women aged fifteen to eighteen need 1,200 to 3,000 Calories. The caloric needs of adolescent males differ from females, and, generally speaking they require more energy. The average eleven- to fourteen-year-old male needs 2,000–3,700 Calories. Between fifteen and eighteen years of age, males require 2,100–3,900 Calories. What all this means is that if you have a larger body and are more active, you need to have more Calories to ensure that you have the energy to perform well. A very active sixteen-year-old girl, for example, might actually need to consume 3,000 Calories a day, while a young man of the same age who is less active might need as few as 2,100. Your caloric needs are therefore tied closely not only to whether you are male or female, but also to whether you exercise and are physically active. Carbohydrates, proteins, and fats are your major sources of Calories.

Carbohydrates

Carbohydrates are the fuel for your body and mind. Most of our energy comes from carbohydrates; one gram of carbohydrates contains four Calories.

Carbohydrates are chains of sugar molecules. Some of these chains are incredibly long and complex, and many carbohydrates don't taste anything like sugar. Since your

26

body can't use most carbohydrates in their original form, food must be converted to glucose—a simple sugar— for your cells to use this food energy. Once your body breaks down the carbohydrates into glucose, the glucose is carried into your cells by a hormone called insulin.

Carbohydrate Myth: *All carbohydrates are bad for me.*
Truth: Not all carbohydrates are the same, and some are much healthier for your body than others. Carbohydrates are found in grain products, fruits, vegetables, other plant products, and even candy. Complex carbohydrates like the ones found in whole-grain foods are much healthier than simple carbohydrates such as the ones found in processed grain products and candy. In complex carbohydrates, chains of sugar are extremely long, sometimes consisting of hundreds of molecules. To digest these complex carbohydrates, your body must break each chain down one sugar at a time. This takes a very long time, supplying your body with a sustained source of energy and giving your body time to absorb the sugars.

The carbohydrates in processed-grain products, like white bread, white rice, and white pasta, have already been broken down into short chains that may be only two or three molecules long. Your body can break all these sugars down at once, causing the level of sugar in your body to spike. In response, your body quickly produces insulin to counteract the imbalance, pulling the sugar out of your bloodstream and into your cells. Usually, however, your body can't burn this flood of sugar fast enough, so it stores the excess sugar as fat—your body's energy storehouse. Once the energy from carbohydrates is converted into fat, it can be hard to use up.

Carbohydrates are an excellent source of energy, but if that energy is not expended, then problems like **obesity** can result. Over time, eating too many simple carbohy-

27

Whole-wheat breads, muffins, and pasta are good sources of fiber.

drates can also increase your chance of getting Type II diabetes, a disease in which your body is no longer able to produce or use the insulin that keeps these sugars from flooding your cells. Type II diabetes can lead to many health complications like heart disease, blindness, kidney disease, obesity, nerve damage, and even coma or death.

Complex carbohydrates are also beneficial to your body because of their high fiber content. When grain products are ***refined*** or processed, they have most of their fiber removed. Fiber is carbohydrates that are so complex your body cannot digest them.

But how can something that your body cannot digest be good for you? Scientists are still investigating what exactly fiber does in your digestive tract, but we know for sure that it is essential for good health. Based on the most recent studies, scientists currently **speculate** that there are two types of fiber, and that each has its own benefits. The first type is *insoluble fiber*. This type of fiber aids digestion by keeping foods moving through your digestive tract. The other type is *soluble fiber*, which helps reduce cholesterol and lowers your risk for heart disease, heart attack, stroke, and some types of cancer. Scientists believe the soluble fiber absorbs cholesterol and fat that is in the digestive tract and carries it back out of the body. Generally, the higher a food's fiber content is, the better. Foods that are high in fiber include broccoli, leafy vegetables, whole oats, brown rice, and the skins of vegetables. Complex carbohydrates like tomatoes, potatoes, and bananas are not high-fiber foods, but they are still very healthy and contain lots of nutrients.

Fats

We often think of fat as always being bad. In part, this is because of North Americans' tendency to consume too much fat, which has contributed to heart disease becoming the number one killer on the continent and obesity becoming a major problem. Fat, however, is simply concentrated energy, and having some fat in your diet is good and necessary. Fat yields nine Calories of energy per gram. Since fat is so energy rich, it takes a lot of work to burn it up, which is why even people who exercise a lot should watch how much they consume. Fat is important, since certain types of vitamins are only soluble in fat and not in water. Nutrients like vitamins A, D, E, and potassium must latch onto fat molecules to be transported around the body and delivered where they are needed. Fat is a building block of muscles, cell membranes, blood vessels, and nerves.

Just as there are different types of carbohydrates, so too are there different types of fats. There are two basic categories of fats: unsaturated and saturated. Unsaturated fats can be further broken down into two categories: monounsaturated and polyunsaturated. Monounsaturated fats and polyunsaturated fats are liquid at room temperature. Monounsaturated fats come from foods like avocados and olive oil. Polyunsaturated fats are found in some grains, nuts, and fish—particularly salmon, lake trout, tuna, and mackerel. The polyunsaturated fats found in these fish are called omega-3 fatty acids. These fats actually reduce your chance of heart disease and lower your blood pressure.

Saturated fats are solid at room temperature and come mostly from animals. Meat, dairy products, and poultry all contain saturated fats. Saturated fats should be eaten in moderation since they contain cholesterol. Cholesterol is a chemical called a lipoprotein that is essential for the construction of cell membranes and nervous-system tissues. Cholesterol is in all animal products. There are two types of cholesterol: *high density lipoproteins* or (HDL) and *low density lipoproteins* or (LDL). LDL cholesterol can be dangerous, because when there is too much of it in your bloodstream, it can build up as plaque on your artery walls. Eventually, this plaque can block the flow of blood and lead to cardiovascular disease, heart attack, stroke, and even death. HDL cholesterol, however, is considered good. The HDL molecule has binding sites—places where the LDL cholesterol latches on. The whole group of HDL and LDL molecules can then be easily flushed from the body.

You can decrease your intake of saturated fats while still enjoying animal-based foods. Instead of drinking whole milk, drink skim milk; instead of eating regular yogurt, eat nonfat yogurt. Make sure you do not exceed the recommended serving size for cheese, and for those times when you need to snack on something cold and creamy, try eating frozen yogurt or ice milk instead of ice cream. Another simple way to reduce the amount of saturated fat you consume is to trim off the extra fat on your meat and avoid eating the skin of poultry. You can also choose eggs from chickens that are fed a special diet to reduce the cholesterol in the eggs they produce. The way we cook our food also affects how much fat it contains. When you fry meat, it sits in and reabsorbs its fat. If you bake, broil, or roast meat on a rack, the fat can drip off and away from the food. Furthermore, poaching your meat or eggs (cooking them in water) can be a great way to reduce fat, because some of the fat will be left behind in the cooking water.

Fat Myth: *Only saturated fats are bad for me. All unsaturated fats are safe because they don't contain cholesterol.*
Truth: It is true that unsaturated fats from plant sources do not contain cholesterol, but cholesterol-free fats, such as coconut oil and palm kernel oil, can be converted into cholesterol inside your body. Some unsaturated fats can be bad for another reason. There is a third category of unsaturated fat, *trans or hydrogenated fats*, that may actually be worse for you than saturated fats. During the process called hydrogenation, hydrogen atoms are

31

Like eating plastic?

To make liquid unsaturated fats into solids, hydrogen atoms are added to the molecules. You could compare this to the production of plastic. Plastic starts out as liquid, petroleum-based oils. The molecular structure of this liquid oil is changed to make it into the solid we call plastic. In fact, some doctors actually compare the stiff, undigestible trans fats to plastic! Many people's love-affair with trans fat has now soured. Some countries are considering banning them from food products all together. The United States, however, has not been nearly so **proactive**. The U.S. Food and Drug Administration (FDA) simply requires that by 2006, all companies list the amount of trans fats on food labels.

Under pressure from different interest groups and consumers, some companies are already listing the amounts of trans fats in their foods, and other companies, like Kraft, have promised to reduce or eliminate the amount of trans fats in their products before regulation becomes mandatory.

added to unsaturated fat molecules. The result is unsaturated fats that stay solid at room temperature.

When the process of hydrogenation was developed, hydrogenated fats became hugely attractive to food manufacturers because they increased the shelf life of food and were very cheap. Many natural fats spoil quickly if they are not refrigerated. Some hydrogenated fats can stay unrefrigerated for months or even years without spoiling! Suddenly hydrogenated fats appeared in everything from breakfast cereal to candy. But companies also promoted hydrogenated fats as a health breakthrough. After all, now people could enjoy margarine on their toast instead of butter (which has saturated fats). Cookies, crackers, pie crusts, fried chicken, and other prod-

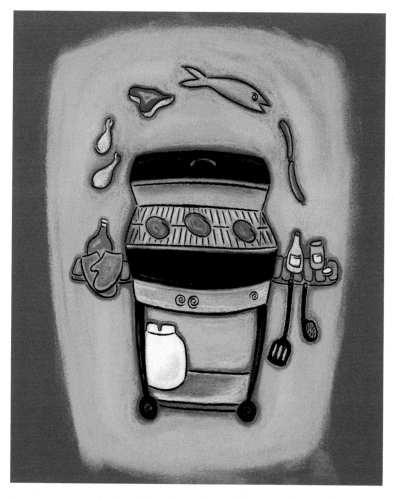

Some meats are higher in fat than others. Fish is usually a low-fat protein source, while fatty red meats may not be as good for you.

ucts that were once made using lard (also a saturated fat) could now be made from unsaturated fat.

It turns out we were very wrong about the health benefits of hydrogenated fats! Not only are they not better for you than saturated fats, many studies now suggest that they are actually worse! Hydrogenated fats do not exist in nature, so our bodies can't recognize what they are or figure out what to do with them. Instead of being broken down into energy and removed from the body, hydrogenated fats get packed away. They clog up the system! They can even build up along the walls of your blood vessels and on the surface of your brain, increasing your risk for heart attack and stroke. They also increase your cholesterol level.

Right now, North American food manufacturers are not required to list trans fats on food labels, so identifying

North American food manufacturers are required to to list some nutrients—but not all—on package labels.

foods with dangerous trans fats can be tricky. To identify trans fats, look on the ingredients label for the words "hydrogenated" or "partially hydrogenated." Anything with these oils in the ingredients list contains trans fats and should be avoided. Unfortunately for all of us, right now trans fats are everywhere! They are found in margarine, candy, donuts, crackers, cookies, snack foods, pies, baking mix, frozen pizza, fast foods like French fries, and many other foods we love.

Proteins

Much of your body is made of proteins—in fact, when a person is fit, protein makes up the second largest portion of his body mass. Your body uses protein to build and repair its tissues; proteins are the building blocks of muscle. However, without exercise, simply increasing the amount of protein you eat will not make you more muscular. Your body can only process a certain amount of protein. Some of the protein will be converted to a sugar called glucose and used as energy. Some will be flushed out of your body. Any protein that is left over will be stored as fat.

For every one gram of protein, your body gets four Calories. Protein comes from both animals and plants. Dairy products, meat, fish, poultry, eggs, grain products, nuts, and **legumes** are all good sources of protein.

Protein Myth: *To get in shape I must eat protein, protein, and more protein.*
Truth: Focusing on one nutrient can get you in trouble. Protein is important to muscles, but too much of it can be

35

hard on your body, especially on your liver and kidneys. If you lead a very active lifestyle, you will need more protein than the average person your age. Most people in North America, however, already consume too much protein and get a lot of that protein from unhealthy, high-fat sources.

If you are trying to strengthen your muscles, eat protein-rich foods within fifteen to thirty minutes after exercising. This way, your body will immediately apply the nutrients to your tired muscles rather than store them as fat. Eat a variety of protein sources rather than just animal products, which can be high in unhealthy fats. Yogurt, orange juice, and a granola bar or a low fat muffin, milk, and an apple are two protein-rich snacks that provide a healthy balance of nutrients.

Food for Thought

Myth: *Food only affects the way my body works, not the way I think.*

Truth: Your brain requires energy too. Not only does food affect your energy levels, which affects how alert you are, it also impacts your mood and your ability to perform decision-making functions. Thinking of your mind and body as separate overlooks the obvious—your brain is an organ of your body. And here's a little food for thought: Studies have shown that the brain uses 360 Calories per day. That is more Calories than it takes to keep your heart and lungs working while at rest; they only need around 330 Calories per day.

Without balanced nutrition, your body's cells, tissues, and organs won't grow and develop properly, you won't be able to think or concentrate to the best of your abilities, and your body and mind simply won't be healthy.

Think about it: why would you want to deny yourself the things that will make you healthy, energetic, and physically strong? When our bodies are fit, our emotions tend to be more upbeat, and life is likely to seem generally more enjoyable. You probably wouldn't deny a good friend something she truly needed in order to be happy, not if it were within your power to give it to her—so be a good friend to your own body and give it the nutrients it needs for good health.

But how much of each food should you consume? This question is the source of great debate. Most North Americans have major misconceptions concerning the types and amounts of foods they should eat. These misconceptions can, in many cases, be traced to the information North Americans have long been taught by government bodies and in school about proper nutrition.

3

MIXED SIGNALS

Food Guides
and Balancing Your Diet

What's one of the greatest influences on the way we think? You might answer our families, our teachers, our friends, or our churches—and all those are true of course. But one of the greatest influences in our world today is something we may not even notice: advertisements. All of us encounter some form of marketing so many times throughout each and every day, that we take it for granted. We may believe that we're not affected by the constant barrage of visual and auditory messages, but our minds can't help but be shaped by that which we hear and see over and over and over and over.

Much of the daily information we receive concerning food comes from advertisements and marketing. In some cases, this information is accurate and helpful, but we should also be wary. The companies that make and sell food are in competition with one another for your business.

Competition has its benefits like increasing the range of choice available and leading to ***innovative*** new products that are sometimes beneficial to our health and happiness. But companies also promote their products at the expense of their competitors. Sometimes a company or industry might promote its products as better than they really are, or try to portray someone else's product as unhealthier than it really is. So, in a world where everyone has something to sell, whom do you trust? How do you know if a particular food is really good or bad for you?

The Food Guides

Governments around the world have tried to offer their citizens reliable information about proper nutrition. The information they gather is summarized in easy-to-follow charts or guides. These guides are a good starting point for understanding the basics of nutrition and healthy eating. Here we will consider two government-based

40

Dairy products include milk, cheese, ice cream, and yogurt.

guides: the USDA's Food Guide Pyramid and Health Canada's Food Guide to Healthy Eating. These guides divide food into different *food groups* and then emphasize these groups as the foundation for a balanced diet. Generally, these food groups are grain products, vegetables and fruits, dairy products, and meat and protein alternatives. These four basic food groups have become the foundation for how North Americans approach a balanced diet. On further consideration, however, we will

41

see why these food groups have become the source of some criticism.

If you live in the United States, probably one of the first things you ever learned about proper nutrition was the USDA's Food Guide Pyramid. From the very first glance, the Food Guide Pyramid tells us something important about a balanced diet. The shape of the pyramid indicates which foods we need the most by putting them at the base—the foundation. The foods we need the least of are put at the top, the narrow pinnacle, of the pyramid. When it comes to the USDA Food Guide Pyramid, the foundation consists of bread, cereal, rice, and pasta, with a daily allotment of six to eleven servings. Vegetables and fruits make up the pyramid's second level. According to

the guide, you should get three to five servings of vegetables and two to four servings of fruit each day. The third level of the pyramid is split down the middle. On one side is the dairy group, which you should have two to three servings of each day. On the other side is the protein group—meat, poultry, dry beans, eggs, and nuts—which should also be consumed two to three times a day. Fats, oils, and sweets, are at the pyramid's pinnacle and should only be used sparingly.

The USDA food pyramid has been a helpful guide to many people, and you've probably seen it many times. The food pyramid, however, has some problems. In many ways it oversimplifies the issue of eating well. Take, for instance, the base level. It contains grain products, a great source of carbohydrates. But as you learned in chapter 2, not all carbohydrates are the same, and some can be very bad for you. Similarly, the USDA food pyramid draws no distinctions between protein sources that are high in saturated fats and those that are low in saturated fats. Furthermore, the pyramid labels all oils "use sparingly." You also learned in chapter 2 that some oils are essential for good health.

Differing from the USDA's pyramid, the Canadian Food Guide looks like a rainbow. Nevertheless, the information contained in this guide is very similar to what's found in the USDA's pyramid. The wide band on the outside consists of grain products. Narrower bands follow, consisting of recommended servings, in descending order, of vegetables and fruits, dairy products, and meat and protein alternatives. One big difference between Canada's Food Guide and the USDA's Food Guide Pyramid, however, is found at the bottom of each rainbow band. Here, there is a recommendation about what types of food best satisfy the nutritional needs that you are supposed to get from each food group. The guide recommends that you choose foods lower in fats more often. When it comes to grain products, it directs people to whole grain or ***enriched*** products more often than those that are processed. For vegetables, the guide suggests that you eat dark green and orange vegetables and fruits more often. In the dairy group, it is recommended that you choose lower-fat products, and when it comes to meat and alternatives, leaner meats, poultry, fish, dried peas, beans, and lentils should be favored over high-fat meats like hamburger or bacon. The Canadian Food Guide also recommends slightly different serving amounts than the USDA's Food Guide Pyramid.

One of the most confusing things about the USDA's Food Pyramid and Health Canada's Food Guide is the serving size. There is a big difference between a serving size and the amount of food you generally help yourself to. One slice of bread is considered one serving. But did you know that a bagel or a bun is considered two servings, and large bagels and buns can even equal three to five servings? One cup of rice or pasta (250 ml) is actually two servings, while a bowl of cereal is between two and three servings. When it comes to cheese, a serving is about an ounce and a half (50 grams). This is about the size of a pair of dice. A serving of meat is three ounces (100 grams), or about the size of a deck of cards. When you pour yourself some juice, do you pour a full glass or half a glass? Half a cup (125 ml) of juice is actually one serving. With vegetables, half a cup of frozen vegetables, one medium-sized fresh vegetable, or one cup of leafy greens is considered one serving. So, although it might seem like the food guides recommend you eat a lot of food, it is actually very easy to consume more than one serving at a time, and even easier to overeat when it comes to foods like cheese and meat. It is also easy to undereat when it comes to vegetables.

Myth: *Snacking is always bad.*
Truth: Part of eating right means feeling great, and let's face it, sometimes this means having something that falls outside of the regular food groups. On occasion, candy, cookies, donuts, and other foods that are generally considered unhealthy can in fact be eaten. It's important to eat these in moderation. It's also possible to find snacks with less fat and salt. Sometimes companies put out products that are similar to the originals, but have fewer Calories in each serving. An option like this can be a good way to snack while reducing the amount of fat, salt, and Calories you would generally get from this type of food. But remember that the suggested serving sizes are usually a lot smaller than the amounts that people help themselves to. If you decide to eat three times the amount of a given food because you're eating the low-Calorie version, you'll undo the low-Calorie benefits. Even some "low-Calorie" foods can still be high in saturated fats, which as we will learn, can have a serious impact on your health.

Whenever you can, try to substitute healthy snacks for unhealthy ones. Healthy snack alternatives are easier to come by than you might think, and they can actually help supplement a balanced diet. Some healthy snack ideas are dried fruit, cheese (only an ounce and a half or 50 grams) on crackers, yogurt, fresh fruit, granola bars, vegetable sticks, rice cakes (you can buy flavored ones), popcorn (just go easy on the butter/margarine and salt), frozen fruit bars, fig bars, and whole-wheat crackers. "Snacking smart" does not have to be ***synonymous*** with "snacking boring."

It's hard to give up snacking, and you shouldn't have to, but if you find that snacking is interfering with your appetite, or you are using snacks as meal substitutes, you

45

Fruits are healthy snacks.

are consuming too much. When you eat when you are not hungry (perhaps you are nervous, sad, or bored), you should try something other than eating. For example, go for a walk, call a friend, turn on some music, or play some yourself.

A Bite of Controversy

Although the USDA's Food Guide Pyramid and Canada's Food Guide can be useful tools, they do not tell the whole nutritional story. They provide only simplified versions of a healthy diet plan. If we really examine nutritious eating, we find that what your body requires is actually much more complex than these guides can easily portray. Both guides are *accessible* and easy to use if you want some quick facts at a glance, but they should be seen as just starting points for understanding your body's needs. Furthermore, you should understand that the pyramid and rainbow were developed decades ago. Though many people still use them, they actually contain some *erroneous* information about proper nutrition.

Nutrition experts at the Harvard School of Public Health realized that the government guides were oversimplified and had some errors. In response, they have tried to create a more accurate guide. The guide is called the Healthy Eating Pyramid, and differs from the other guides in important ways. First, the new guide does not recommend "servings" of food. Instead, Harvard's nutritionists looked at the average amount of food people actually ate, and used this information to make a recommendation of how many times a day a person should eat each type of nutrient. Harvard's pyramid also differs from the other guides in that it doesn't just concentrate on food. It also concentrates on lifestyle. Therefore, the base of Harvard's pyramid is not grain products; it's exercise! Harvard's nutritionists recognized that, even if you ate the ideal types and amounts of food, you still would never be healthy if you did not exercise. At the root of eating properly, therefore, is a balanced lifestyle, which includes physical activity as well as eating properly.

The second level of Harvard's pyramid is whole grains. The pyramid recommends whole-grain foods be eaten at most meals. As we saw, whole-grain foods are generally better for us than grain products that have been processed. Unlike the other food guides we discussed, Harvard's food pyramid recognizes that not all grain products are the same, and that some should be avoided.

> Lifestyle, or your way of living and behaving, is often about choice. You might get ideas about your lifestyle from others around you, including your friends and family. Ideas might also come from the media, for example, from the types of products you see advertised. But you probably also find that when you choose from all these sources, mixing and matching them, you create something that uniquely reflects who you are. Included in lifestyle are choices about proper nutrition and exercise.

Another significant difference in Harvard's pyramid is its handling of fats and oils. Unlike the USDA's pyramid and Health Canada's rainbow, which relegate all fats and oils to the smallest portion of your diet, on Harvard's food pyramid, certain fats and oils actually share grain products' level! As we discussed in chapter 2, some fats and oils are actually good for you and essential for proper physical and mental functioning. Olive, soy, corn, and some other vegetable oils, and fatty fish (for example,

Servings of food can be difficult to determine!

salmon) are examples of fats can actually be good for you. According to Harvard University, fats appear on the second level of the pyramid, not because you should eat them in the same quantities that you eat grain, but because more than one-third of the average North American's daily Calories come from fat. The Harvard food pyramid, therefore, puts healthy oils on this rung to emphasize the importance of these Calories that come from healthy fat sources.

Above grains and oils are vegetables, which should be eaten in abundance, and fruits, which should be eaten two to three times a day. After fruits and vegetables come nuts and legumes, which should be eaten one to three times a day. Fish, poultry, and eggs make up the pyramid's fifth level and should be consumed at most, two times each day. The sixth level contains dairy products or calcium supplements, with the recommendation that these be consumed one to two times a day. Finally, at the top of the pyramid, is the "Use Sparingly" section. This section includes red meat and butter (sources of saturated fats) and simple carbohydrates such as white rice, white bread, potatoes, white pasta, and sweets.

The Harvard Healthy Eating Pyramid is one of the best food guides available today, but it has been shocking to many people. It demonstrates that the average North American diet is completely upside down! How many times have you heard the term "meat and potatoes" to refer to the North American meal? Far from being the basis for a healthy diet, these are the very things that you should be avoiding. On the other hand, the foods that North Americans consume the least of, whole-grain foods and vegetables, are the foundation of healthy eating.

Another way to see if you are eating the correct amounts of different nutrients is to think about the percentage of your diet each nutrient fills. According to a recent study released by the National Academy of Sciences, 45 percent to 65 percent of your daily energy needs should be met by carbohydrates. The next largest portion of your Calories, about 20 percent to 35 percent, should come from fat. It may surprise you to know that the smallest amount of your Calories, about 10 percent to 35 percent, should come from protein.

Precisely how much of each nutrient you should consume depends on factors like your age, size, sex, and activity level. A teen's body is different from an adult's or child's body. During adolescence, the body is growing and changing rapidly. As a teen, you may need more protein and fat than adults need to help build your body tissues. If you are very active, you will need more carbohydrates for energy than a person who is inactive. If you are a male, you may need more protein than a female. Adapting your diet for different stages of development ensures good health today, but also increases your chances of maintaining strength and fitness in the future.

Good nutrition, however, doesn't stop with carbohydrates, fats, and proteins. You need many other nutrients to be healthy and happy. Many of these come in the form of vitamins and minerals.

4

The Other Essentials

Vitamins, Minerals, and Water

Your body can't function on energy alone! Thousands of chemical reactions are taking place in your body at any given moment, and these vital functions could not occur without the other essential nutrients: vitamins, minerals, and water. Keep in mind that it is almost impossible to get enough of any single vitamin or mineral from just one source. You should eat a variety of the foods that supply each of the vitamins and minerals.

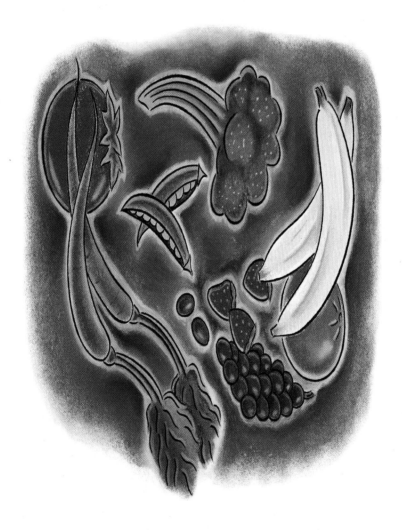

Fruits and vegetables are rich in vitamins.

VITAMINS

Vitamins only make up about 0.00002 percent to 0.005 percent of your diet, but without their presence, normal health cannot be maintained. You get most of your vitamins through your food, either naturally or through vitamins added to many packaged foods. Each vitamin aids specific body functions. Here are some of the most important vitamins and descriptions of what they do in your body.

VITAMIN A

Vitamin A comes in two basic forms: retinol, which comes from animals, and carotene, which comes from plants. Vitamin A is important for the immune system—the body system that fights infection. It's also important for eyesight and the growth and repair of body tissues like mucus membranes, bones, teeth, and skin. It is fat soluble, which means that it is transported throughout the body by joining up with fat molecules. Vitamin A is found in green and yellow vegetables, fish oil, and egg yolk.

THE B VITAMINS

The B vitamins include B_6, B_{12}, thiamine (B_1), riboflavin (B_2), niacin (B_3), pantothenic acid (B_5), and folic acid (B_9). They play diverse roles throughout your body including keeping your vision healthy, improving your cardiovascular health, maintaining bone strength, and preventing depression, fatigue, and irritability. Folic acid can help prevent birth defects like spina bifida, a serious condition in which the spinal column remains incomplete, causing damage to the central nervous system. It is recommended that women of child-bearing age who are sexually active take a folic acid supplement. All B vitamins are water soluble, meaning that they are transported through your body by fluids rather than fats. B vitamins are found in eggs, grains, dairy, meat, and beans.

VITAMIN C

Vitamin C, or ascorbic acid, is necessary for maintaining healthy teeth, gums, and bones. It also helps your body absorb iron (an important mineral), promotes healing, reduces scar tissue, improves your immune system, and strengthens your blood vessels. In addition, it is an antioxidant, a substance that some scientists believe slows the aging process in our cells. As an antioxidant, vitamin C also helps prevent dangerous **nitrates** from converting into cancer-causing substances. Vitamin C deficiency can cause bleeding gums, anemia, tooth decay, and a disease called scurvy. Vitamin C is water soluble. Citrus fruits, melons, dark leafy greens (like spinach, kale, and mustard greens), cauliflower, sweet potatoes, and tomatoes are just a few of the many sources of vitamin C.

VITAMIN D

Vitamin D, a fat-soluble vitamin, is commonly found in fish oils, liver, and egg yolk and helps the body **metabolize** minerals like phosphorus and calcium. As such, the nutrient is essential for the health of your bones. You may not need to get vitamin D from food sources, however, because your skin can actually produce it as long as you are getting enough exposure to sunlight. Be careful though! Although some sunlight is essential for good health, UVA and UVB rays in sunlight age your skin and

Many fruits contain vitamin C.

greatly increase your risk of developing skin cancer. You should wear sunscreen every day, especially if you have light skin. If your skin is dark, you have some natural protection, but sunscreen is still a wise choice.

VITAMIN E

Vitamin E is an important fat-soluble antioxidant. It could help reduce your risk of cardiovascular disease and cancer. Vegetable oils and nuts are good sources of vitamin E. In North America, people generally consume enough vitamin E from a typical diet. Something to keep in mind, however, is that a low-fat diet can decrease the amount of vitamin E in your body. Remember, mono- and polyunsaturated fats are beneficial for your health. Almonds, hazelnuts, and sunflower seeds are particularly good sources of vitamin E. Fish, nectarines, pumpkin, and dark leafy greens are other sources.

VITAMIN K

Vitamin K is fat soluble and aids the clotting ability of your blood. Without adequate vitamin K, a body will bruise more easily and more severely, and if cut, a wound will bleed more profusely. Most of your vitamin K is actually produced by bacteria that live in your intestines. Food sources of vitamin K include cauliflower, cabbage, dark leafy greens, soybeans, and liver.

Vitamin Myth: *It is possible to get all the nutrients I need from vitamin pills and other nutrient supplements.*
Truth: Taking a multivitamin every day cannot replace the range of nutrients your body gets from healthy eating. When you eat unhealthily, taking a pill will not bridge the nutritional gap. In fact, the body will still lack many of the

important things that help it stay healthy and alert. While multivitamins contain some vitamins and minerals, a healthy diet ensures a wide range of nutrients, including those minerals that exist in trace amounts in food. Taking a multivitamin is a good idea, but only as a precaution to guarantee you are getting all you need on a daily basis— kind of like a backup in case you missed something in your diet, never as a substitute for healthy eating.

Minerals

Minerals are also essential for your body's proper development and function. Like vitamins, minerals are usually taken in through your food. Some minerals may also be present in the water that you drink, especially if that water comes unfiltered from a well or spring.

Calcium and Phosphorus

Calcium and phosphorus are particularly important for the health of your bones, teeth, muscles, and nerves. Without calcium, our bones will not develop the strength necessary to support us throughout our lives. Calcium is especially important during the teen years when our bodies enter a critical growth period. In fact, about three-quarters of your skeleton develops while you're a teen! A lack of calcium during this period can cause long-term problems like *osteoporosis*. Excellent sources of calcium include dairy products and dark leafy greens. Most doctors also recommend that all women, who are more susceptible to osteoporosis than men are, take calcium supplements.

59

Like calcium, phosphorus is also found in dairy products. Phosphorus aids in the formation of vitamin D, which is needed for calcium absorption. Balance is important, however, because too much phosphorus depletes your calcium levels.

SODIUM, POTASSIUM, AND MAGNESIUM

Sodium, potassium, and magnesium are all essential for proper cellular, nervous system, and muscular functioning, as well as to maintaining a regular heartbeat. Potassium might protect against stroke, and magnesium is necessary for strong bones.

The main source of sodium is sodium chloride, table salt. As you may already know, too much sodium can be dangerous and might increase your blood pressure and your risk for heart disease. Potassium is found in bananas, legumes, and a wide range of other foods like meat, poultry, fish, and fruits. Good sources of magnesium are dark leafy greens, nuts, and soy products.

ZINC

Zinc is important for the normal functioning of the immune system, wound healing, *fetal* development, hormones, and sperm production. Zinc is found in oysters and other seafood, red meat, poultry, whole grains, beans, nuts, and dairy products.

IRON

Another important mineral is iron. Iron is extremely important because it helps transport oxygen throughout the body. Without enough iron, a person can suffer from anemia, the result of which might be pale skin, ***apathy***, and fatigue. Women generally require greater amounts of iron than men because they lose blood as part of the menstrual cycle. As a result, the iron needs for young women increase during their teenage years, in particular between the ages of eleven and eighteen. Some very good sources of iron include cooked dry beans and other legumes, enriched and whole-grain products, shellfish (clams, mussels, shrimp, and oysters), red meat, and spinach. People who drink too many carbonated beverages, drink alcohol, smoke, skip meals, or consume too much salt may risk iron deficiency.

WATER

Water may not seem like a nutrient, but it is! It is essential to your body's metabolism, temperature regulation, and vitamin, mineral, and nutrient transport. Water also helps your body excrete the waste products that are produced from digestion and metabolism. When you become thirsty, your body is already at a relatively advanced stage of dehydration, meaning that it lacks enough water to function as well as it should. When you perspire from hot weather or exercise, your brain may not detect your level of dehydration for some time. To avoid dehydration, it is important to consume at least 8 cups (about 2 liters) of fluid a day. Water is found not only in the fluids we drink but also in the foods we eat. Fruits, vegetables, nuts, and even baked goods all contain water.

It is one thing to know which nutrients are important for your body, but it is another thing to know how much of each nutrient you should get. Even though vitamins and

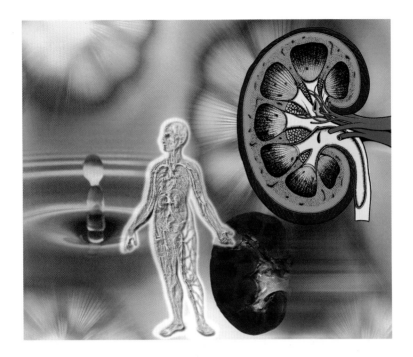

Water helps keep your kidneys healthy.

minerals are essential to good health, they are also ***potent*** chemicals, and many of them can be toxic if consumed in excessive amounts. Here are some of the daily nutrient amounts recommended by the National Academy of Sciences for people between eleven and eighteen (the amounts vary, depending on age and whether you're male or female):

Vitamin A:	800–1,000 µg
Vitamin E:	8–10 mg
Vitamin K:	45–65 µg
Vitamin C:	50–60 mg
Thiamin:	1.1–1.5 mg
Riboflavin:	1.3–1.8 mg

Niacin:	15–20 mg
Vitamin B_6:	1.4–2.0 mg
Folate:	150–200 µg
Vitamin B_{12}:	2.0 µg
Iron:	10–15 mg (This is the one nutrient where girls need more than boys.)
Zinc:	12–15 mg
Vitamin D:	5 µg
Calcium:	1300 mg
Phosphorus:	1250 mg
Magnesium:	240–410 mg

When you were younger, your parents told you what to eat. They probably tried to encourage you to eat the foods that would provide you with the various nutrients you needed to grow. But you're older now, and you've begun making your own decisions about what you eat and don't eat. Learning what your body needs to be healthy is an important part of becoming a responsible adult. Taking care of yourself makes sense if you want to be happy and enjoy life.

But making wise food choices isn't the only thing you need to do if you want to be healthy. You also need to make certain your body gets the exercise it needs.

5
GET MOVING

Staying Fit for Your Life

Heaving her backpack onto the counter, Sarah opened the fridge, grabbed a can of soda, and searched for something to eat. She poked at a dish of leftover salad, but after a few half-hearted forkfuls, she ripped

Beginning an exercise program can be difficult—but once you've found the right one for you, you may find it's lots of fun.

open a package of chips instead. She just didn't feel like eating veggies. She was tired after a long day at school, and all she wanted to do was flop down in front of the television.

Sarah trudged upstairs, and sat down at the computer. She went through her usual ritual: e-mail first, open up the instant messenger, and check the news sites. "Obesity Epidemic in Schools" read one headline. She clicked on the story. "Changing lifestyles have created new opportunities and challenges for young people and their health. The Internet, video games, television, and even homework all compete with physical activity for the time and attention of today's adolescents." Sarah read on. "But new challenges face educators today. With budget cuts to education, classes in physical education have declined. School boards everywhere must find ways to deliver the core academic courses on smaller budgets. This means that gym classes for many levels have been eliminated."

Sarah shook her head. She hated gym class, so it wouldn't bother her if her school cut it from her schedule. In fact, she'd be relieved. Running around in gym shorts was embarrassing, especially now that she'd put on some weight.

"If young people are to escape our society's newest epidemic," the article continued, "they may have to develop new lifestyles. Exercise is an important aspect of fighting obesity. Doctors recommend a minimum of thirty minutes strenuous activity three times a week, but if. . ."

Sighing, Sarah turned away from the computer and clicked on the television instead. Soon, she'd have to do her homework, but right now, she just wanted to rest. The last thing she wanted to do was exercise.

Some Exercise Basics

The problems associated with lack of exercise have been the subject of studies and news programs in recent years. As new activities have taken the place that physical activity traditionally held, teens are less active now than they were in years past. Increasing the severity of the problem are cuts to physical education classes. Not only has this eliminated the only opportunity for exercise many teens had but it also diminished the prominence of exercise as a key to a healthy lifestyle. There are now fears that as lack of exercise spreads over a greater number of years, conditions like obesity, heart disease, and arthritis will increase sharply, and at earlier ages.

Physical activity is the foundation of feeling great and can lead to more energy, increased strength, better endurance, and more flexibility. The benefits of exercise are also long lasting, and by staying active, you can increase your life expectancy and reduce the chance of contracting problems like cardiovascular disease. Even moderate amounts of exercise have been shown to have a positive impact on stress levels and mood, improving a person's overall quality of life. Many people also find that their self-esteem and self-image improve by getting into shape.

Broadly speaking, there are two categories of exercise, aerobic and anaerobic. Aerobic exercise increases your heart and breathing rates. This type of exercise can come from activities like rowing, basketball, swimming, jogging, brisk walking, skating, hiking, soccer, dancing, aerobics, cross-country skiing, cycling, and hockey (particularly during practices). Aerobic exercise must be sustained for at least twenty minutes, but preferably thirty minutes, before your body begins to experience

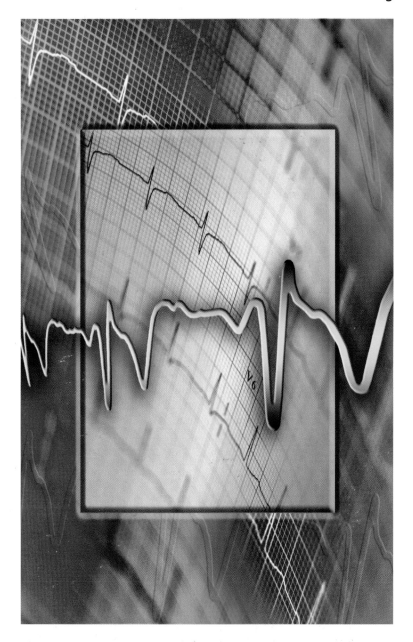

Aerobic exercise gets your heart moving faster.

significant health benefits like strengthening your heart and lungs, and before your body begins burning fat. Remember, fat is your energy storage system. It's your body's protection against starvation—like a food savings account in case food stops coming in—so your body will use all the other energy available to it before it delves into the fat reserves.

When you participate in aerobic exercise, check your pulse, or heart rate, to see if you are working hard enough to get the benefits from the exercise. Teens should aim for a maximum heart rate of 140 to 170 beats per minute. To check your pulse, use your index and middle finger (avoid using your thumb, because it has a noticeable

pulse of its own) and press them lightly on the inside of your wrist. You should feel the blood pumping beneath your fingers. If you are having trouble, another good place on the body to check for your pulse is on the neck just below and to the inside of your jawbone. Count the number of times you feel your pulse in a minute—or do it for six seconds and multiply it by ten. Raising your heart rate for sustained amounts of time strengthens your heart. When your heart is strong, it pumps more blood with each beat. A strong heart can move the blood your body needs in fewer beats than an unhealthy heart can. One way to gauge the strength of your heart is to check your heart beat when you are at rest. A resting heart rate that falls between sixty and one hundred beats per minute is considered normal for teens and adults. The lower your resting heart rate, the stronger your heart is. Well-trained athletes typically have resting heart rates between forty and sixty beats per minute. Another way to check is to see how long it takes your pulse to return to its normal rate after exercise. The quicker your heart rate returns to normal, the better cardiovascular shape you are in.

Anaerobic exercise is exercise that strengthens your muscles but does not have cardiovascular or respiratory benefits. While exercise needs to be sustained to increase heart strength, anaerobic exercises usually involve short bursts of intense resistance-based activity to strengthen muscles. Anaerobic exercise is a good complement to aerobic exercise because the stronger and larger your muscles are, the more energy they will require and the more calories they will burn. Anaerobic activity has other benefits besides improving your muscle strength. It also strengthens your bones, tendons, and ligaments while it improves your muscle tone. Your endurance may also benefit from this type of exercise since it will take longer

for your stronger muscles to tire. Many people who practice strength training find that their overall body shape and physical performance improve. Whether you are strength training for issues of physical appearance or not, there will be many benefits to your health.

To become stronger, muscles must work against resistance. Anaerobic activities provide that resistance to your muscles. One of the most common forms of anaerobic activity is weightlifting, but there are many other ways to achieve anaerobic exercise. Push-ups, leg lifts, and abdominal crunches all build strength. Working out in the water through swimming, water aerobics, water-weight training, and other water-based activities can be aerobic if engaged in a way that raises your heart beat for the required amount of time, but these can also make great anaerobic workouts because the water provides resistance to all your muscles. Water exercise is also very beneficial for people who are extremely out of shape, have an injury, or are older as takes pressure off of the joints, especially the knees and hips. People who might have avoided or not been able to exercise because of pain may find water exercises to be an answer.

When engaging in anaerobic activities like weightlifting, teens in particular should be careful. Evidence suggests that lifting heavy weights before a person is fully grown can damage the long bones' growth plates, stunting the development of the body. People who are still growing are also more susceptible to bone fractures, muscle strain, and damage to the body's joints. Strength training using moderate amounts of weight is generally not harmful. Power-lifting and weight training, however, can be dangerous and should only be engaged in by people who are completely physically mature. For most people, growth stops between ages sixteen and eighteen. Yet many young people, particularly young men, begin to body build while in high school. Perhaps this is because many of the sports that are most popular with North Americans are sports in which size and weight are an advantage—football, wrestling, and hockey are striking examples. Nevertheless, despite a teen's desire to grow bigger, and in spite of the pressure that is often added from coaches and perhaps even parents, serious weightlifting is best left until adolescent development has fully run its course.

Anaerobic exercise and aerobic exercise complement each other because together they will improve your metabolism—or the rate at which your body consumes energy—so that even while at rest, your body burns more Calories. Muscles require more energy to maintain than body tissues like fat require. Through a combination of aerobic and anaerobic exercise, your proportion of body fat and muscle will change, with fat decreasing and muscle increasing. This causes a beneficial chain reaction in which your metabolism and Calorie-burning capabilities also increase. When your metabolism works efficiently, your body can make more effective use of the vitamins, minerals, and other nutrients you consume.

So What Type of Exercise Should I Choose, and How Much of It Should I Do?

So how do you know how often you should exerecise ? Traditionally, doctors have recommended that people engage in a minimum of twenty minutes of moderately vigorous aerobic activity at least three times a week. This means that every other day, you should be taking part in aerobic exercise.

However, this recommendation came with the assumption that people would engage in many other physical activities (like walking or riding a bike to school, participating in gym class, playing basketball or other games with friends, gardening, and even cleaning) every day. It turns out, however, that North Americans are becoming more inactive all the time. **Sedentary** pastimes have reduced drastically the amount of time the average person spends moving. New studies have shown that moving— plain and simple—is vital to good health, and a planned aerobic exercise regime should be an *addition* to your other daily movement and activity. If you spend most of every day engaged in sedentary activities, then twenty minutes of exercise three times a week is not going to be enough to make you healthy. You need not work out seven days a week, but you must be active every single day.

Part of your daily physical activity should also be anaerobic. Muscle is a body tissue for which the saying "use it or lose it" really applies. If you are not engaging your muscles every day, they quickly deteriorate and get converted to fat for storage. Daily strength-building activities are also vital to building and maintaining strong bones. You probably don't have time, however, to do strength-building exercises for every part of your body every day. Alternating workouts between your upper and lower body is a good approach to daily anaerobic exercise. This approach also reduces your chance of injury.

Despite knowing the benefits, many people still find it difficult to exercise. Why? As we saw in Sarah's story, the busy schedules of many teens can make it a challenge to find the time to exercise. Furthermore, exercise requires physical work, and, let's face it, this work isn't always pleasant. But exercise does not have to be a chore. When you were a little kid, you probably exercised all the time. You were always running around and playing. You probably never stopped to think that what you were doing was actually good for you. Chances are you were having too much fun. Similarly, physical activities that you take part in as a teenager can be as fun as they are good for you. Understanding why an active lifestyle is good for you can help you choose which activities best suit your particular fitness goals—whether it's losing weight, gaining strength, increasing your energy level, or improving your cardiovascular health. Thinking about the full range of exercise options available can also help you choose a fitness routine that appeals to your own sense of fun, making sure that exercise becomes an enjoyable part of your leisure time. If you enjoy doing it, you'll be more likely to stick with it.

Whether you like participating in group activities or prefer to do things on your own, there are many options available to you. Competitive people who enjoy the company of others might very well enjoy playing competitive sports. Someone more introverted might enjoy cycling or kayaking. Even people who face health issues can adapt exercise to their needs. For example, if you suffer from epilepsy, activities like scuba diving or rock climbing would be dangerous and highly inadvisable, but fun activities like trail hiking and cross-country skiing could be perfectly safe. If you suffer from a common condition like asthma, you can work with your doctor to find treatments that will allow you to participate in activities. Everyone should consult her doctor before beginning a new form of exercise.

Lack of time and a dislike for physical work are certainly not the only things that hold teens and other people back from exercising. For many people, self-consciousness, low self-esteem, and embarrassment are huge barriers to starting an exercise plan. A person might be out of shape, overweight, uncoordinated, or any number of other things that could make her apprehensive about playing a sport or taking part in an activity. If this is your situation, remember that there are all kinds of ways to exercise. You can exercise on your own. Starting out by walking is one very good way to reduce your weight. Exercising in private by skipping rope or using home exercise equipment like a stationary bike are other ways to overcome this problem. A brisk walk can burn Calories, strengthen muscles, and can be an aerobic workout. Finally, if you still feel self-conscious, remember that your choice to exercise is about you, not about what others think. So making decisions for and about yourself is totally within the province of your power. Besides, adversity almost always seems bigger in our heads

If extreme sports aren't for you, experiment until you find an activity that's a good match for your personality. You'll find there's something for everyone.

than it really is. The truth is, probably no one will ever even notice the things about which you feel self-conscious. Everyone has insecurities, but insecurities shouldn't get in the way of good health. Even better, it is through exercise that many people discover their bodies really are capable of strength and good health. In the face of this discovery, many insecurities will quickly fade.

Another important thing to remember is that you don't have to start out big. If you have not been exercising regularly, do not start your first day by trying to run a marathon or break world records. Instead, make a steady effort to increase your strength and stamina over time. Even simple physical activities expend energy and are important steps on the road to fitness.

Calories Burned Per Hour
for Selected Activities

Activity	Calories/Hour
Sleeping	45
Walking	352
Dancing	317
Scrubbing floors on all fours	387
Low Impact Aerobics	352
Basketball Game	563
Canoeing (moderately hard)	493
Golf	281
Hockey	563
Rock climbing	563
Running	563
Skating	493
Cross-country skiing (light)	493
Tennis	493
Cycling (leisurely)	281
Mowing Lawn	387
Swimming	422

Get Moving

The number of Calories burned per hour varies depending on your body size. Look at the different activities in the chart on page 78. The numbers of Calories burned per hour are estimations based on a person weighing 155 pounds (70 kg). When calculating how many Calories you would burn for any of these activities, take your personal body weight and divide it by 155. Then multiply this number by the number of Calories that a 155-pound person would burn over the course of an hour. For example, if you weigh 195 pounds, the equation would read $195 \div 155$. This would give you a factor of 1.258. Next, take the total number of Calories a person weighing 155 pounds would burn for a selected activity and multiply that number by the factor you calculated in the first step. In the case of basketball, a 195-pound person would burn 563 calories x 1.258, or 708.254 Calories for one hour of basketball.

Look at the activities in the adjacent chart and make the necessary calculations to discover approximately how many Calories you would burn for different activities. Notice how activities of similar intensity burn roughly equal numbers of Calories.

Getting fit and staying active require a balance between different types of exercise. Finding a routine that fits well for you is important. Any type of physical activity is better than no physical activity, but to get optimal results you should strive to mix aerobic and anaerobic exercise. Find something you enjoy—and make it a lifelong habit!

6

EXERCISE-RELATED RISKS AND INJURIES

How to Avoid Them

*N*o *pain, no gain.*

You've probably heard that saying more than once.

But the truth is, exercise shouldn't hurt!

The Best You Can Be

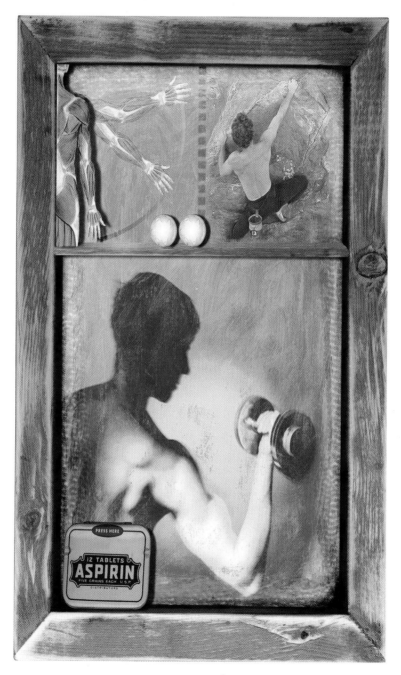

Lack of exercise can be a vicious circle: the less we move our bodies, the weaker they become. The weaker our muscles, the more tiring it becomes to do even simple exercise. The more tiring exercise becomes, the less apt we are to make time for it in our lives. You get the picture.

But the circle works the other way as well. Once you begin exercising regularly, you'll find your body has more energy. As you have more energy, you will find exercising more enjoyable. As exercise becomes more fun, you'll be more motivated to make time for it in your life—and the more often you exercise, the stronger your muscles will become. . . . It takes some effort to form new habits. But the payoff is worth it.

Of course, as in most things, moderation is the key. Don't set yourself goals that are impossible to reach. Not only will you become discouraged, but you're more apt to injure yourself as well.

While you might feel some discomfort when exercising, especially when you begin a new form of exercise, anything that is seriously painful means that you are pushing your body too far. This can seriously strain your heart, lungs, and muscles and can cause injuries. Instead, beneficial exercise should be moderate, consistent, and sustained. How do you know if you are pushing yourself too hard? In aerobic exercise, a good gauge is: Can you talk? If you can only force out one or two words at a time, you are working too hard; you should be able to engage in light conversation. In anaerobic exercise, the test is: does it hurt? If so, you are doing too much. Injuries like torn muscles, ligaments, and tendons can result.

While taking part in an activity, the adrenaline rush you experience and your mind's preoccupation on the tasks at hand might cause you to tune out the pain your body is feeling. However, once you have stopped exercis-

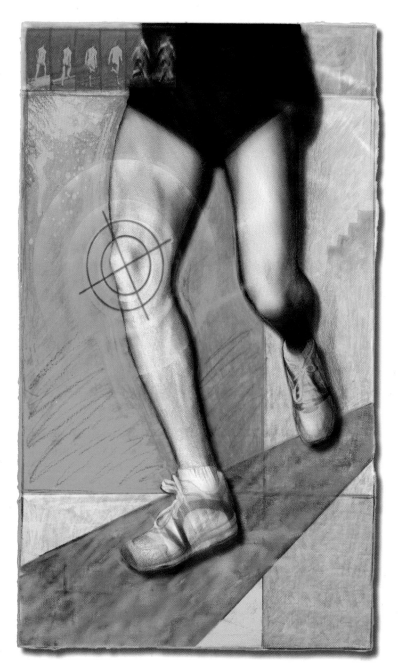

ing, you might discover that serious damage has been done. Most sports injuries involve damage to your muscles or bones. The musculoskeletal injuries occur most frequently in the joints, such as ankles, knees, hips, elbows, and shoulders, that absorb much of the shock from exercising. High-impact activities like running and some sports like basketball can hurt the cartilage and soft tissues in these body parts.

In the long term, damage to joints can lead to painful inflammation and stiffness known as arthritis. This disease typically does not show up until later in life, but much of the strain starts earlier in life. The good news is that usually sports injuries can be avoided by using well-fitting equipment, such as proper shoes, warming up through stretching your muscles before taking part in high-impact or aerobic activities, and exercising on soft surfaces (for example, grass, dirt trails, or flexible wood or carpeted floors) rather than on hard surfaces (such as concrete sidewalks, paved roads, or inflexible floors).

Some of the most common injuries experienced by athletes are shin splints, stress factures to bones, blisters, muscle cramps, strains, and sprains. The sensation that accompanies shin splints is aches and pains along the front or inside portion of the leg between the knee and ankle caused by the muscle tearing from the shin. Activities involving a lot of running can cause shin splints. If you suffer from shin splints, you should rest the muscle and treat it with ice or anti-inflammatory medicine. Some causes of this type of injury are pronation (putting too much weight on the inside of your feet when you run) and a strength imbalance between the muscles in your leg. Very often taking a break can heal the injury, and strengthening the muscles in your legs over the long term can help to keep shin splints a thing of the past. To ensure that shin splints do not happen again, it is important to stretch the calf muscles. Running on a different surface or changing the type of shoes you wear can also help solve the problem.

Stress fractures sometimes have the same symptoms as shin splints. These are tiny fractures along the surface of the bone, which can occur when you exercise. After a while, as your muscles become tired, their ability to absorb the shock from running is diminished, and the strains become absorbed by your bones.

A common injury from ill-fitting shoes and other sports equipment is blisters. These are often painful, but usually are not very serious. Having well-fitting sports equipment is the best way to prevent this injury. Muscle cramps can also be painful, but for the most part they are not particularly serious. Without a proper warmup included in your exercise routine, the chance of suffering a muscle cramp is increased. Cramps are, essentially, involuntary muscle contractions. If your muscles are fatigued, you have a shortage of magnesium, calcium, potassium, or other important minerals, are dehydrated, or have exercised heavily, you might experience cramping during or after exercise. The best ways to treat cramps are through heat, pressure, massage, and slow stretching (for leg cramps, remember "toes to the nose": stretch your leg and point your toes up toward your nose). If your muscles continue to spasm, or you cannot explain the source of the cramps, it is recommended that you consult a doctor.

Strains involve injury to your muscle or tendon. In their mildest form, strains can be a sore pulled muscle. In more severe forms, they can be a complete tear of the muscle and tendon. A sprain is a stretched or torn ligament. Like strains, sprains can be relatively mild, or they can involve severe injury and pain. In both cases, a person suffering from a strain or sprain will feel pain, stiff-

A recent study by a team of Yale University researchers found that some weightlifters may be at risk of rupturing the ***aorta*** during workouts. When you lift a weight, the muscles in your body contract, causing a rapid, extreme increase in your blood pressure. The heavier the weight, the stronger the muscular contraction is; the stronger the contraction, the larger the spike is. In a number of cases, this blood-pressure spike has caused the lifter's aorta to tear open. The team of researchers believes that people who already have weak arteries due to ***genetic*** or other factors are at the greatest risk for this type of injury. Further research is under way.

ness, and swelling, and will have difficulty moving the muscle. To treat these injuries, it is recommended that you apply "R.I.C.E.": *R*est, *I*ce, *C*ompression, and *E*levation. By resting the muscle, you reduce the chance of aggravating the injury. Ice can help reduce swelling and inflammation, both of which can prolong the healing process. Compressing the injured area by lightly but firmly wrapping something like an elastic bandage around it can reduce pain and swelling by preventing the build up of fluids in the area surrounding the injury. Elevating the injured area can also reduce fluid accumulation.

As we discussed earlier, weightlifting can be an especially risky activity for teens. The heavier the weights you use, the more serious an injury you are likely to sustain. Some of the injuries associated with weightlifting include broken bones, internal injuries, dangerous spikes in blood pressure, and ruptures of major arteries. To avoid injuries, learning the proper technique from a trainer or coach is ***mandatory***. Furthermore, when weightlifting, always remember the number one rule: Never lift without a spotter—another person who can get help if you are injured or support the weights if you should falter. In weightlifting, muscle fatigue happens extremely quickly. Imagine bench-pressing a significant amount of weight and finding your arms buckling. Without a spotter, your chest could be crushed. Besides, having a buddy spot you also means you can get that extra bit of encouragement, something that everyone needs from time to time.

Taking the time to put in the proper effort both before and after exercising can help prevent injury and discomfort. When exercising, make sure that you begin by warming up your muscles by stretching. Before you begin aerobic activity, take five minutes to loosen up your joints and warm your muscles by going for a walk. There are few things worse than waking up sore from the previous day's physical activity and finding yourself unable to exercise because you ache too much. Having a "cool-down" walk after exercising also helps to prevent discomfort and allows your heart and lungs to transition gently back to a lower pulse and breathing rate. You should also finish an exercise session with another round of stretching. After all, exercise is great way to reduce stress and improve your mood, so taking precautions to make sure that you get these benefits should be part of your exercise routine. Besides, stretching will increase your flexibility, which is part of having a healthy and strong body. It can also be very relaxing, and many people enjoy taking part in stretching activities. Yoga, martial

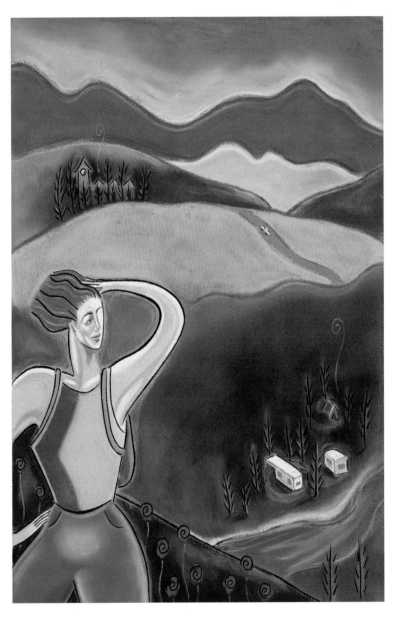

Many people find that exercisie helps them relax and handle tension better.

arts, Pilates, gymnastics, and ballet all emphasize stretching in their strength training.

Sometimes, no matter what precautions you have taken, you might be injured. Medical attention should be sought if pain persists. It is also important to rest the part of the body that is hurt to ensure that it heals properly. Most important, once you recover, do not be discouraged, but continue exercising.

When you exercise correctly, the chances of being injured are low, while the benefits to your health, happiness, and energy level are very high. Taking part in physical activities is a necessary component to a healthy lifestyle. When you begin exercising, start slowly and work your way toward a longer and more vigorous routine. The chances of being injured are greater when you are just setting out after leading a sedentary lifestyle. Try low-impact exercises like swimming, yoga, water aerobics, brisk walks, and relaxed cycling before jumping into high-impact activities like running, step aerobics, and jumping rope. Also, don't feel that you have to stick to a type of exercise you don't enjoy. Remember that exercise should be fun, so if you do not like the first set of activities that you choose, try other ones. You will probably find that once you give exercise a chance, the opportunities and options for activities are almost endless. Just as healthy eating involves consuming a wide variety of foods to ensure you are getting all the nutrients you need, healthy exercising involves performing a wide variety of activities to ensure your body is getting all the types of movement it needs.

Myth: *People who struggle with their weight are couch potatoes and eat fatty foods.*
Truth: People naturally have different shapes and sizes. While diet plays a role in how we look, so do genetics.

90

There are three broad categories of body types: ecto-morphs, endomorphs, and mesomorphs. The category, or combination of categories, that describe your body type is determined by the genes you have inherited from your parents. An ectomorph has a lean build and gener-ally does not have a very muscular appearance. A person with this build seems to be able to eat a lot of food with-out ever gaining weight. An endomorph tends to have a rounder build with a higher proportion of body fat, and often finds it difficult to lose weight because of a slower metabolism. A mesomorph is someone whose build is between these extremes. In fact, the first part of the word, meso, means "in between" or intermediate. Meso-morphs burn calories easier than endomorphs, but not as easily as ectomorphs. They are also better able to gain muscle than ectomorphs. Sometimes a person's weight has less to do with their eating habits and lifestyle than with their genetics, and a person with one body type could eat less and be more active but still appear heavier than a person with another body type.

Keep your focus on health rather than appearance. Listen to your own body, and don't push it further than is good for it.

Our society is full of messages about how we should appear—but if we pay too much attention to these out-side voices, our perceptions may become skewed. In-stead of caring for our bodies responsibly, the way we would care for any other valued possession, we may de-velop habits that are less than healthy. They may even be destructive.

7
GOING TOO FAR

True or false?

*Being thin means being
healthy.*

False! Contrary to popular
belief, just because a person is thin does not mean

that person is active or healthy. If you are an ectomorph, you might find it hard to be anything other than thin, even without exercising. Regardless of how much you eat, it might seem impossible to put on a few pounds. While others might envy you for this, it can be frustrating if your goal is to gain a little bit more muscle. It can also lull you into thinking you are healthy even if you're not. If you are an endomorph, you might have the opposite situation; you might not look thin, but you might be perfectly fit and healthy.

For many people, becoming thin is a major goal of exercise and proper nutrition, but the biggest benefit is being healthy. Furthermore, being too thin can be a serious health problem. If you eat fewer Calories than your body needs and you do not exercise, you might be thin, but your body will be under strain, and this can lead to health issues that range from feeling tired and worn out to problems like irregular heartbeats.

Maintaining a healthy balance in your lifestyle—that is, eating food from all the food groups and getting a mix of exercise so that your body is working at its most efficient—is central to getting and staying happy and feeling great. Getting yourself into shape should also be about having fun. It is okay to want to use exercise to improve your appearance, but sometimes in the quest for perfection, people can take their pursuit of fitness and healthy eating too far. From eating so little that normal body weight is ignored to compulsively over-exercising, ***detrimental*** results will follow. Knowing how to recognize the symptoms of illnesses that relate to nutrition and fitness is important. Eating disorders are common among young people, particularly among young women. Three of the most common eating disorders are anorexia nervosa, bulimia, and binge eating.

Anorexia Nervosa

Anorexia nervosa is a psychological illness more commonly known simply as anorexia. It involves an obsession with losing weight, rapid weight loss, refusal to eat or the willingness to only eat certain foods (and these in nutritionally inadequate amounts), and excessive exer-

More young women suffer from anorexia than young men, perhaps because girls feel greater pressure from peers as well as society to conform to a particular body image.

cise often to the point of collapse. One major psychological component of anorexia is that even though a person can appear underweight to those around her, she continues to perceive herself as fat.

More women suffer from anorexia than men, and some experts speculate that the media's targeting of young women is to blame. Women are barraged by media images promoting body types that are not achievable for most young women. Women may feel pressured to conform to these images, and anorexia may result. Young men also feel significant amounts of pressure to conform to certain media images, but since the celebrated male body types are muscular and not as waif-like as those promoted for females, a significantly smaller number of young men suffer from anorexia. Estimates put nine out of ten sufferers of anorexia as women. Young men, however, are at increasing risk of falling prey to this disease.

Anorexia can result in ***emaciation***, irritability, depression, bad breath, dehydration, fatigue, weak bones, kidney damage, heart problems, muscle loss, hair loss from the head, and hair growth all over the body (the body's emergency measure to retain heat and stay warm). Starved of essential nutrients, the body's production of sex hormones falls, and, in the case of a woman, her menstrual period can stop. Anorexia can also cause death, and various studies estimate that anywhere from five to 20 percent of sufferers will die from the disease.

Bulimia Nervosa and Binge-Eating Disorder

Another fairly common and serious eating disorder is bulimia nervosa. Like anorexia, people with bulimia consider themselves overweight, fear food, ***abhor*** fat, and loath gaining weight. The difference between the two diseases is the way that they manifest themselves. While anorexia involves self-starvation and weight loss, bulimia is characterized by binge eating followed by purging, or forcibly ridding the body of what was eaten.

Binge eating is consuming a large amount of food in a very short span of time. In one sitting, or binge, a person eats many times the Calories a person typically eats in a whole day. A person suffering from bulimia feels out of control during these binges. Once the bingeing stops, however, guilt, depression, and shame set in. Through forced vomiting, laxatives, excessive exercise, fasting before the next binge, or taking diet pills, a sufferer of bulimia attempts to cleanse herself of the binge and avoid the weight gain the extra Calories could cause. Many people with bulimia seem physically healthy and emotionally happy to outside observers. Even family members and close friends may have no idea their loved one is suffering from a serious disease. The person, however, is secretly in turmoil. Quietly keeping her eating habits secret, a person with bulimia is often depressed, lonely, and suffers crises of self-confidence and hidden anger.

> A person with an eating disorder may be constantly obsessed with the effort to lose just one more pound. In fact, many people use their weight as a gauge for judging their progress toward a healthier body. However, weight can be misleading, and striving for an ever-lower weight can be dangerous. As your body becomes stronger and healthier, the proportion of fat decreases while the proportion of muscle increases. Therefore, you could weigh the same as you did before but actually be healthier and trimmer. In fact, when you become healthier and more muscular, you could even end up weighing more than you did before, but you won't look larger than you did before.

Since the pattern of bingeing and purging differs so significantly from the self-starvation of anorexia nervosa, a person with bulimia can appear perfectly healthy to

A person with bulimia can appear perfectly healthy.

those around her. She may not even lose weight. Yet, like anorexia nervosa, serious health problems are caused by this eating disorder, which can even lead to death. Included in the side effects of bulimia are damaged teeth (as the acid from vomiting eats away at the valuable

99

Both anorexia and binge eating can damage your heart.

enamel on the backs of teeth), bad breath, burned esophagus, irritated lungs, kidney damage, muscle weakness, dehydration, and even seizures. Purging can also deplete the body of important minerals like potassium and sodium. These nutrients help to regulate the heartbeat. In fact, depletion of these minerals can lead to heart failure, the most common form of death among people with bulimia. A person can suffer with bulimia for years and, without warning, die suddenly and unexpectedly. Like anorexia nervosa, the depression, distorted body images, and health complications should not be ignored. Instead, the issues surrounding the illness should be dealt with by medical professionals.

Binge-eating disorder is similar to bulimia in that the person engages in uncontrollable binges. It is different, however, in that the person does not purge afterwards. Some of the major risks of binge-eating disorder are serious weight gain and health conditions like cardiovascular disease, diabetes, arthritis, and other conditions caused or aggravated by obesity.

Body-Dysmorphic Disorder

Besides eating disorders, there are other conditions that can cause an unhealthy approach to fitness and nutrition. One of these is body-dysmorphic disorder. Feeling some dissatisfaction with your body is normal. Wanting to improve your body's fitness is a **laudable** goal. Yet, if you want to change your body, think of it from the perspective of improving your physical health. Having a healthy body image means accepting the uniqueness of your body, acknowledging the differences between your body and other bodies, and remembering that there is no such thing as a perfect body.

Persistent negative feelings of unhappiness and dissatisfaction about one's body can be the sign of a psychiatric disorder known as body-dysmorphic disorder. This disorder is relatively rare and involves a person obsessing on a part of the body that she perceives as flawed. These flaws are usually at least partially imagined. A person suffering from body-dysmorphic disorder is, nevertheless, convinced that her misperception is reality.

Worrying about a part of your body is not necessarily a symptom of this disorder. Focus on the part of the body perceived as flawed must be so severe that it significantly impacts the person's life and interferes with her ability to

A person with body-dysmorphic disorder may perceive that his body is flawed, even though others may see nothing wrong with him.

function normally, diminishing her quality of life. A person with body-dysmorphic disorder thinks of her physical flaws, no matter how slight, as serious deformities. Obsessing over the idea that others are preoccupied with her deformities, is another aspect of the illness. She may also be convinced others are talking about her or laughing at her "defect."

North Americans are more likely to suffer from this disorder than people from other parts of the world. The image-oriented culture that permeates our society is perhaps the greatest single reason for this. Interestingly, men and women tend to suffer from the disorder in approximately equal numbers. The most common parts of the body over which people with body-dysmorphic disorder obsess are the teeth, mouth, eyes, nose, scars, eyebrows, wrinkles, and hair. A man will sometimes also focus on the size and function of his penis, while women might focus on their breasts and hips.

A person with body-dysmorphic disorder may become obsessed with fitness, nutrition, or other tactics for improving her "flaw." No matter how hard she tries, however, the flaw will not disappear because she is seeing it with her mind, not with her eyes. A person with this disorder should seek professional medical expertise. The problem is psychological and, as such, requires treatment that deals with the root cause of the illness.

Steroid Abuse

Steroid abuse is a destructive fitness-related activity that disproportionately affects young men. Just as young women can feel pressure to relentlessly slim down to the point of damaging their health and happiness, young men can feel a pressure to "get big," "get ripped," and "bulk up." Driven to increase their body size and make it more muscular, young men sometimes move beyond healthy levels of body building and good nutrition and try to take shortcuts like anabolic steroids. Female athletes, too, can feel pressure to take steroids in the hopes of improving their physical performances and strength.

Anabolic steroids are synthetic chemicals that behave similarly to male sex hormones like testosterone. People use these chemicals because they spur muscle growth. Physicians sometimes prescribe steroids to treat various illnesses, but most of those wanting to increase their muscle mass acquire them illegally. Dangerous side effects can result from the abuse of anabolic steroids. Male characteristics like body hair and a deeper voice can develop. This side effect is more detectable in women than in men, but there are many other side effects as well. Men who use steroids commonly begin to grow breasts and have their testicles shrink. Aggressiveness, rage (sometimes known as "'roid rage"), male-patterned baldness, and acne can occur in both men and women who use steroids. Other complications include heart failure and liver cancer. Some effects of steroid use, like baldness, can be permanent. The tendency to take on some of the characteristics of the opposite sex evidences the severe disruption that steroids pose to the body's own natural hormone production. When the body is saturated with chemicals that mimic its own hormones, the endocrine system, the system that manufactures hormones, shuts down. People who take steroids, therefore, experience their own body ceasing to produce hormones. It is not clear what, exactly, the long-term effects of shutting down the body's endocrine system will be.

Steroid use has become increasingly high profile. From disgraced Olympic athletes to professional football players, weightlifters, and body-builders, the tempting allure of an easy fix has raised the hopes of many who only later have found their reputations and health dashed upon the barren reality of steroids. Despite these public displays of the risks associated with steroids, use among teens increased throughout the 1970s and 1980s. In the 1990s, steroid use among young men leveled off, but during the same period, use among teenage girls doubled. Most women who use steroids are athletes, while generally, nonathletes who use steroids are males. Most athletic organizations have banned steroids, and

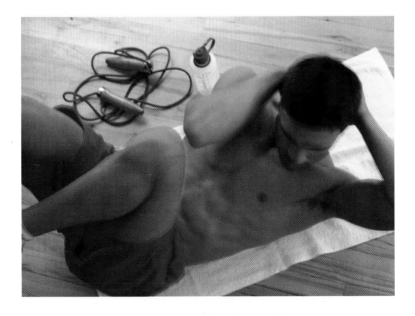

The best way to build muscles is with exercise, rather than steroids.

education programs have emphasized how dangerous these chemicals are. But another reason for the leveling off of steroid use is probably the result of the popularity of legal supplements like creatine.

Legal Supplements

Many people assume that just because legal supplements often contain promises of all-natural ingredients they are safe. But these supplements often have their own side effects. People who body build and power lift are particularly interested in ways that will help them bulk up. Since protein is the major building block of muscles, you might not be surprised to learn that most nutritional supplements have high protein contents. Teenage boys in particular want to find ways to make their bodies bigger and stronger—and many turn to protein supplements in the belief that these will be safe for their bodies. Unfortunately, in spite of the legal availability of many of these substances, taking supplements to enhance performance and strength can be very risky behavior.

Some supplements appear to increase the strength and size of athletes who use them. Creatine is the most popular of these supplements. However, this substance can have serious side effects. In vertebrates, creatine is a natural result of protein processing. Evidence suggests that this substance plays an important role in supplying energy to muscles, and this is likely related to the enhanced performance that many athletes experience from its use. But these positives might actually be outweighed by negative effects.

Unlike medicine, nutritional supplements are not regulated by either the U.S. Food and Drug Administration (FDA) or Health Canada. Lack of government regulation means that when it comes to issues of safety and efficacy, there is no way to determine reliably the claims made by the manufacturers of these supplements. In addition, there have been no long-term studies documenting the effects of prolonged supplement use. Among the risks reported by athletes are increased susceptibility to strains, tendonitis, muscle cramps, nausea, diarrhea, weight gain, and even seizures. Furthermore, both protein and creatine supplements can harm your liver and kidneys. It is unclear what the full effects of creatine are and what levels (if any) can be taken safely, and who should or should not use it. As a result, it is a bad health decision to use legal supplements without the advice of a doctor or other medical professional.

DIETING

There are many misconceptions about dieting and its benefits to health. With obesity and related health problems, such as Type II diabetes and heart disease, escalating in North America, losing weight is a good idea for many people. Instead of eating a nutritionally balanced diet and engaging in beneficial exercise, however, many people turn to dieting for a quick fix to their weight issues. Losing weight, if it is done improperly, can be harmful to a person's health.

The number one thing for you to know about dieting is that in the long run, DIETS DO NOT WORK! Having a healthy diet is one thing—going on a diet is quite another. The popularity of dieting remains strong in image-conscious North America, however. Today, one-third of all women in the United State and about one-fifth of American men are dieting in one form or another. Yet, most of them will find it difficult to keep off the extra pounds that they shed, and at the same time, they expose themselves to serious long-term risks. Ninety-seven percent of people who lose weight through dieting will gain the weight back within five years. In fact, three-quarters of people do so in the first year, and many people gain back even more weight than they lost. These statistics show us that diets do not help achieve permanent weight loss, but only provide a temporary ***reprieve*** from being overweight. Dieting alters your body's nutrient levels and

A low-carb diet does not include healthy foods like whole-grain cereals and fruit.

metabolism, sometimes leaving people even more susceptible to later weight gain.

One of the trendiest forms of dieting is the high protein/low-carbohydrate diet first made famous as the Atkins diet. By eating foods high in protein and even fat—like eggs, hamburger, and roast beef—and simultaneously cutting carbohydrate consumption down to almost nothing, a person can lose weight. However, the cost of this weight loss might be high and could lead to high cholesterol levels, cardiovascular disease, kidney damage, sore joints, increased cancer rates, and bad breath, among other side effects. While the high protein/low carbohydrate diet might be fashionable, consult with your doctor before trying this weight-loss option.

High protein/low carbohydrate diets are just one kind of diet a person might use to try to lose weight. But all fad diets, whether it is the grapefruit diet, the no-fat diet, or the liquid-only diet, deprive your body of balanced nutrition. Eating in this manner is especially harmful to teens.

Because the teenage years are so important to growing and developing into a healthy adult, your body needs the mixture of fats, carbohydrates, proteins, and other nutrients that ensure normal health during these years. Dieting can lead to malnourishment, slowing you down and causing dizziness, fatigue, mood swings, hair loss, and headaches.

Furthermore, as you diet, your body attempts to preserve energy by slowing down your metabolism. As you decrease the amount of Calories consumed, your body attempts to ward off starvation by slowing the rate those Calories are burned. People who suffer from undernourishment develop more slowly, hit puberty later, and have weaker bones. Prolonged dieting can cause permanent damage.

A balanced diet includes plenty of fresh vegetables.

Instead of eating and exercising well, some people attempt to mimic the effects of dieting through the use of pills. The pills alter the normal physical functions of your body by changing your metabolism rate, suppressing your appetite, or preventing nutrient absorption. Dieting pills can be addicting, or cause heart ***arrhythmias***, dizziness, seizures, and other very serious problems. Some diet pills can only be obtained through a doctor's prescription or illegally because of the dangers associated with them. Pills containing the chemicals ephedrine, phentermine, and fenfluramine have been withdrawn from the market because of the health complications and deaths they have caused. Other pills contain high amounts of caffeine, so much so that health risks from caffeine overuse have been reported. Another category of diet pills are so-called herbal products. Companies often market these pills as being all natural, implying that they are safe. However, these products have also been linked to health complications like serious liver damage. Kava-kava, for example, has been banned in Canada, and in the United States the FDA has published warnings about it. "All-natural" products are still strong substances and can have serious side effects.

Unhealthy methods of weight control and fitness training can be life threatening. Illnesses like anorexia nervosa, body-dysmorphic disorder, bulimia nervosa, and steroid use are all medical problems. These behaviors are highly risky, and if you or a person you know is experiencing any of these problems, do not be afraid to get help. When it comes to issues about the body, sometimes the only solutions come from trained medical professionals.

Instead of dieting or using steroids, diet pills, or supplements, a balanced diet with exercise is the most effective way to lose weight, get healthy, and stay happy. All this may seem like an ideal lifestyle that's impossible to actually achieve. But if you set small, easy-to-reach goals, you really can change the way you live.

The important thing is to take that first step.

8

YOU CAN GET THERE FROM HERE

Setting and Achieving Goals

We all feel tired and unmotivated sometimes. Even the most dedicated athlete can have days when she doesn't feel like lifting a finger. So how do you get and stay motivated? How do you keep exercising and eating well even when it feels impossible to do?

The first thing to remember: you don't have to be perfect all the time! There's no need to run five miles every single day or never eat an unhealthy food that you enjoy. The key to health is moderation, and moderation is also a key to sticking to your healthy lifestyle. If you never give yourself a day off or never allow yourself a tasty snack, frustration can quickly set in, and you'll be more likely to abandon your healthy lifestyle.

Goal setting is also an important part of maintaining a healthy lifestyle. Without setting goals, achieving significant advances in your health and fitness can be difficult. Goals fall into two categories: short-term goals and long-term goals. Short-term goals are those that can be satisfied in the near future. An example of a short-term goal is, "Tomorrow I will jog for half an hour," or even while jogging, "I'm going to make it to the end of the block." Short-term goals can be ends in themselves, but they can also be steps toward a long-term goal. Long-term goals are those that you want to achieve in the more remote future. Some long-term goals might be "I'm going to swim a mile," or "I'm going to achieve a resting heart rate of 65 beats per minute." Progress toward long-term goals is usually slow and may be imperceptible at first. If you become too focused on lofty long-term goals, you may become frustrated and give up.

To achieve long-term goals, you should have intermediate short-term goals that you can achieve on a regular basis. These will be rewarding, let you know you are making progress, and help to keep you motivated. If your long-term goal is to get into shape and stay healthy, then a short-term intermediate goal might be to eat no trans fats today. This goal can be achieved in one day, helps you toward your long-term goal, and gives you an immediate sense of accomplishment. If your long-term goal is to be able to run for an hour, then your short term goal might be to run for ten minutes every other day for a week. Say to yourself that you are going to reach the ten-minute goal, that you will do your best, and that you know you can do it. Then give it a try. When you reach the goal, take a moment and feel proud of yourself. Even if you do not achieve your objective on the first try, by thinking positively, you are creating the conditions that make good things happen.

Once you achieve your ten-minute goal, sets your sights at fifteen minutes. If you set a goal that's too high for the immediate term, don't be afraid to step back and set a smaller goal. It is easier to accomplish a series of short-term goals than to accomplish one huge goal all at once, and the repeated rewards of accomplishing short-term goals will keep you motivated and on track.

A realistic short-term goal might be eating a salad every day.

The Best You Can Be

Positive thinking is another essential part of a healthy lifestyle and is a good technique for helping you accomplish your goals. Thinking positively has the added benefit of improving your mood and self-esteem. From time to time, all of us experience negative thoughts. But when negative thinking chokes out positive emotions, making a conscious effort can help you overcome them. Just as your body needs physical nutrients and exercise to remain healthy, your mind also needs emotional nutrients and positive mental exercises. Affirmations are positive mental and emotional exercises. If you are finding it difficult to stick to your goals, or are suffering from bouts of self-doubt, positive affirmations may help. They can be a great way to help you keep up your efforts, or to "psych" you up before tackling a challenge.

Psych yourself up for exercise by tracking your progress. Always think in positive terms rather than negative.

Affirmations are positive statements you say about yourself to yourself. By focusing on good qualities, you can actually begin to change your thought patterns and improve the way you think about yourself. Try this exercise. Make a list of ten nonphysical, positive characteristics that describe you. For example, you might be honest, generous, warm, friendly, open, considerate, funny, or gentle. Repeat each characteristic to yourself three times while you are alone. Try looking in a mirror at least some of the time that you do it. Over time, the negative phrases that run through your head will be replaced by these positive ones. This may sound simplistic, and you may feel silly doing it, but exercises like these can actually have a significant impact on your self-esteem. After all, if you say or hear something enough times, no matter what it is, you'll probably begin to believe it, so make sure the phrases you repeat to yourself every day are positive ones.

It is not always easy staying positive as a teenager. The ways your body is changing may make you feel awkward and insecure. Along with changes to your outward appearance, you may also experience changes in mood. As a teen, the emotions you experience are often strong—the positives are *really* positive, and the lows can be *really* low. These mood changes can be exhausting, and staying positive in the face of them is difficult. But making the effort to be positive will have payoffs as things slowly begin to change, improving your mood. Believing in yourself is essential to achieving your goals.

Another way to improve self-esteem is to spend your time with positive people. Sometimes this is easier said than done. As a teenager, your increasing freedom also gives you more of an ability to pick the company you keep, especially when it comes to choosing who your friends are. We all know of people who seem to be down

117

A well-balanced diet includes a wide variety of foods.

about almost everything and everyone. Negative people can often bring us down with them, harming our self-esteem in the process. By sticking to the company of people who are positive and encouraging, your attitude toward yourself and others can shift to a more positive position. Not only will your self-esteem rise, but by hanging around people who are friendly and supportive, you will likely find yourself having more fun! Finding others who enjoy the same physical activities you enjoy can also be a great way to keep yourself motivated and on track. It's often easier to exercise if you have an exercise buddy.

When it comes to health and happiness, you need to be proactive. No one else can make you eat right, get in shape, maintain your current fitness level, have a positive attitude, or develop high self-esteem. By picking up this book to get information about fitness and nutrition, you have already begun to be proactive about taking control of your own health and happiness. Now you have some knowledge to apply to your health efforts. The next step is to set some small, clear, and achievable goals. Think positive. Enlist some friends or family members as supporters in your efforts to get healthy. Keep in mind that physical health is a key component of mental and emotional health.

> Success is not final. Failure is not fatal. It is the courage to continue that counts.
>
> —Winston Churchill

More than anything else, remember that you can do it! You're growing up now, and you have the power to shape your own life. As you work with your own body's abilities, taking one step at a time, you can create healthier habits that will last a lifetime.

Douglas, Ann. *Body Talk: The Straight Facts on Fitness, Nutrition and Feeling Good About Yourself!* Toronto, Ontario: Maple Tree Press, 2002.

Duden, Jane. *Vegetarianism for Teens.* Mankato, Minn.: LifeMatters, 2001.

Gaede, Katrina, Alan Lachica, and Doug Werner. *Fitness Training for Girls: A Teen Girl's Guide to Resistance Training, Cardiovascular Conditioning and Nutrition.* San Diego, Calif.: Tracks Publishing, 2001.

Jukes, Mavis. *The Guy Book.* New York: Crown Publishers, 2002.

Kirgerger, Kimberly. *No Body's Perfect: Stories by Teens about Body Image, Self-Acceptance, and the Search for Identity.* New York: Scholastic Inc., 2003.

Libal, Autumn. *Can I Change the Way I Look? A Teen's Guide to the Health Implications of Makeovers and Beyond.* Philadelphia, Penn.: Mason Crest Publishers, 2005.

Luciano, Lynne. *Looking Good: Male Body Image in Modern America.* New York: Hill and Wang, 2001.

McCoy, Kathy, and Charles Wibbelsman. *The Teenage Body Book.* New York: The Berkley Publishing Group, 1992.

Pipher, Mary. *Reviving Ophelia: Saving the Selves of Adolescent Girls.* New York: G. P. Putnam's Sons, 1994.

Pope, Harrison G., Katharine A. Phillips, and Roberto Olivardia. *The Adonis Complex: The Secret Crisis of Male Body Obsession.* New York: The Free Press, 2000.

Salter, Charles A. *The Nutrition-Fitness Link.* Brookfield, Conn.: The Millbrook Press, 1993.

Youngs, Jennifer Leigh. *Feeling Great, Looking Hot, and Loving Yourself!* Deerfield Beach, Fla.: Health Communications Inc., 2000.

American Council on Exercise
www.acefitness.org

American Dietetic Association
www.eatright.org

DMOZ: Open Directory Project
dmoz.org/Health/Fitness/Organizations

The Harvard Healthy Eating Pyramid
www.hsph.harvard.edu/nutritionsource/pyramids.html

Food and Nutrition Information Center
www.nal.usda.gov/fnic

Health Canada
www.hc-sc.gc.ca

Mind on the Media
www.mindonthemedia.org

The National Eating Disorders Association
www.nationaleatingdisorders.org

NIH Clinical Center: Facts about Dietary Supplements
www.cc.nih.gov/ccc/supplements

Nutrition.Gov
www.nutrition.gov

Nutrition Navigator: A Rating Guide to Nutrition Web-
sites by Tufts University
navigator.tufts.edu

The President's Council of Physical Fitness and Sports
www.fitness.gov

U.S. Department of Health and Human Services: National Institutes of Health
www.nih.gov

Publisher's note:
The Web sites listed on these pages were active at the time of publication. The publisher is not responsible for Web sites that have changed their addresses or discontinued operation since the date of publication. The publisher will review and update the Web sites upon each reprint

abated Lessened, eased.

abhor Hate; loathe.

accessible Approachable; reachable.

aorta (ay-OR-tah) The main artery coming from the heart.

apathy Lack of strong feelings one way or another.

arrhythmias (a-RITH-me-uhs) Irregular heartbeats.

detrimental Obviously harmful.

emaciation (ee-MASE-ee-a-shun) The physical wasting away of a body.

enriched Made better by adding something.

erroneous Incorrect; wrong.

facilitate To make easier.

fetal Relating to an unborn vertebrate.

genetic Relating to the genes, packets of hereditary information within each living cell.

hormones Products of living cells that circulate throughout the body and affect the activity of other cells.

idealized Attributed unrealistically positive characteristics to someone or something.

innovative Done in a new way.

laudable Worthy of praise.

legumes (le-GOOMS) Plants that have seed pods, including peas and beans.

mandatory Required.

media Methods of mass communication.

metabolize To provide energy for vital processes through chemical changes in living cells.

misconceptions Misunderstandings.

molecules The smallest particles of a substance.

nitrates Chemicals found in tobacco smoke, burned food, smog, and preserved and smoked meats like bacon.

obesity A condition characterized by excessive body weight.

osteoporosis (AH-stee-oh-poh-roh-sis) A disease in which bones become brittle and fracture easily. Although it can be found in men and in all races, major risk factors include being a thinly built, white female.

potent Extremely strong or effective.

proactive To act in anticipation of what might happen.

refined Without impurities or unwanted materials.

reprieve A temporary suspension of a condition.

sedentary Doing or requiring much sitting.

speculate To theorize or guess.

steroids Hormones that can increase growth, muscle mass, and stamina.

synonymous (si-NON-i-mus) The same as.

PICTURE CREDITS

Artville pp. 10, 24, 38, 64, 77, 82, 84, 92, 100
BrandX pp. 62, 69
EyeWire pp. 22, 28, 33, 41, 46 52, 54, 80, 89
iDream pp. 49, 57, 110, 112
Image Source pp. 94, 96
PhotoAlto p. 12
Photodisc pp. 17, 18, 34, 42, 66, 70, 72 99, 102, 105, 108, 115, 116, 118

The individuals in these images are models, and the images are for illustrative purposes only.

Christopher Hovius is a graduate of Queens University in Kingston, Ontario. He is a freelance author who is enjoying living an active, heart-smart lifestyle in Vancouver, British Columbia. He would like to thank Autumn Libal for her contributions to this book.

Mary Ann McDonnell, APRN, BC, is an advanced practice nurse, the director of the clinical trials program in pediatric psychopharmacology research at Massachusetts General Hospital, has a private practice in pediatric psychopharmacology, and is a clinical instructor for Northeastern University and Boston College advanced practice nursing students. Her areas of expertise are bipolar disorder in children and adolescents, ADHD, and depression. Mary Ann is one of a small group of advanced practice nurses working in pediatric psychopharmacology research and practice, who has a national reputation as an expert advanced practice nurse in the field of pediatric bipolar disorder, ADHD, and depression. She sits on the institutional review board and the research education committee at Massachusetts General Hospital and is a lecturer for local and national educational conferences on bipolar disorder, depression, and ADHD.

Dr. Sara Forman graduated from Barnard College and Harvard Medical School. She completed her residency in Pediatrics at Children's Hospital of Philadelphia and a fellowship in Adolescent Medicine at Children's Hospital Boston (CHB). She currently is an attending in Adolescent Medicine at CHB, where she has served as director of the Adolescent Outpatient Eating Disorders Program for the past nine years. She has also consulted for the National Eating Disorder Screening Project on their high school initiative and has presented at many conferences about teens and eating disorders. In addition to her clinical and administrative roles in the Eating Disorders Program, Dr. Forman teaches medical students and residents and coordinates the Adolescent Medicine rotation at CHB. Dr. Forman sees primary care adolescent patients in the Adolescent Clinic at CHB, at Bentley College, and at the Germaine Lawrence School, a residential school for emotionally disturbed teenage girls.